*We have not begun to live
until we conceive of life as a tragedy*

William Butler Yeats

Also by Simon Callow

Being an Actor
Charles Laughton – A Difficult Actor
Shooting the Actor
Acting in Restoration Comedy
Orson Welles – The Road to Xanadu
The National – The Theatre and its Work 1963-1997

Simon Callow

Love is
Where it Falls

An Account of a Passionate Friendship

NICK HERN BOOKS
London

A Nick Hern Book

Love is Where it Falls
first published in Great Britain in 1999
by Nick Hern Books Limited
14 Larden Road, London W3 7ST

Reprinted 1999

A CIP catalogue record for this book
is available from the British Library

ISBN 1 85459 257 2

Typeset in Garamond Antiqua by
Country Setting, Kingsdown, Kent CT14 8ES

Printed and bound in Great Britain by
MPG Books Limited,
Bodmin, Cornwall PL31 1EG

This book is dedicated to J., B. and M.,
in the name of love

And he went back to meet the fox.

'Goodbye,' he said.

'Goodbye,' said the fox. 'And now here is my secret, a very simple secret: it is only with the heart that one can see rightly; what is essential is invisible to the eye.'

'What is essential is invisible to the eye,' the little prince repeated, so that he would be sure to remember.

'It is the time you have wasted for your rose that makes your rose so important.'

'It is the time I have wasted for my rose – ' said the little prince, so that he would be sure to remember.

'Men have forgotten this truth,' said the fox. 'But you must not forget it. You become responsible, forever, for what you have tamed. You are responsible for your rose . . . '

'I am responsible for my rose,' the little prince repeated, so that he would be sure to remember.

From *The Little Prince*
by Antoine de St-Exupéry
translated by Katharine Woods

Nothing I have written has been more directly personal than the present book. It passed through many drafts before reaching its final form, and in order to achieve anything like an objective view of it, friends – a small army of them – have been bombarded with successive versions. Their reactions have played a crucial part in shaping the book, and I thank them all deeply, with particular gratitude to David Hare, Martin Sherman, Peter Gaitens, Angus Mackay and Ann Mitchell. I should also like to thank Nick Hern, editor, publisher and friend, for equal quantities of patience, encouragement and perception during the book's seemingly interminable evolution, and Maggie Hanbury, my agent, for her entirely correct conviction at a crucial point that there was a ways yet to go.

S.C.

Part One

Part One

1

Somewhere in a safe in a room in a solicitor's office in London is a small urn, containing the ashes of a remarkable woman: Peggy Ramsay, the most famous play agent of her time. It is nearly seven years since she died, and I have still not summoned up the courage to do what she asked me to do: to take her ashes to the cemetery of San Michele in Venice and scatter them there. Why can I not do this simple thing for her?

*

It was a sunny summer's morning in 1980 when for the first time I ascended the spindly staircase, festooned with posters of theatrical triumphs past, that led to Margaret Ramsay Ltd, in Goodwin's Court, off St Martin's Lane, in the centre of the West End of London. I had come to collect a copy of a play in which I had acted a couple of years before, in the theatre, and which I now hoped to persuade the BBC to do on television. Straight ahead of me, at the top of three flights of stairs, was the door with the agency's name on it, under several layers of murky varnish. The last thing I expected or wanted to do was to talk to Peggy Ramsay herself, but when I opened the door, there she unmistakably was, sitting at a desk – or rather *on* one – as she flicked through a script, almost hitting the pages in her impatience to make them turn quicker. Her skirt was drifting up round the middle of her thighs to reveal knee-high stockings. Hearing me enter, she looked up with an expression which seemed to mingle surprise, amusement and challenge, as if she'd been expecting me but had rather doubted I'd have the courage to come. It was a curiously sexy look.

'Hello,' I said, 'I'm – '

'I know *exactly* who you are, dear,' she said. 'Tell me,' she continued, as if resuming a conversation rather than beginning one, 'do you think Ayckbourn will *ever* write a *really* GOOD play?'

'It's an interesting question,' I replied nervously, slightly inhibited by the fact that I was at that moment appearing in a play by the author under discussion, and that he was by far the most successful client of the woman asking the question. 'You'd better come in,' she said, calling over her shoulder for 'tea and *kike*' to one of the young women in the office, as she ushered me into what was evidently her private office. Adjusting and readjusting her skirt – a flowery item, beige, silk and diaphanous – she kicked off her shoes and seated herself at her desk, while I settled down on the sofa.

'Ah, that sofa . . . ' she murmured, mysteriously, with many a nod and a smile, as she absent-mindedly combed her fine golden hair. The room had an air of glamorous chaos about it, half work-place, half boudoir. There were shelves and shelves of scripts right up to the ceiling, their authors' names boldly inscribed in red down the spine: in one quick glance I saw Adamov, Bond, Churchill, Hampton, Hare, Rudkin. There were books, in great tottering piles; awards, both framed and in statuette form; posters (all of Orton, Nichols in Flemish, Mortimer on

4

Broadway); plants everywhere, trailing unchecked; discarded knee-high stockings, scarves, hairbrushes, make-up bags, mirrors and hats: huge, wide-brimmed, ribbon-toting hats, four or five of them, draped over the furniture. The air was headily fragrant, confirming the room's overpoweringly feminine aura.

In the midst of it all was Peggy, clearly the source of both the glamour and the chaos. She was now answering the telephone in a startlingly salty manner. 'Well, you'll just have to tell them to fuck off, dear,' she was saying to one caller, 'I shall tell Merrick that we *must* HAVE a million' to another. 'But your play's *no* GOOD, *dear*,' she cried, to a third, informing me in an entirely audible aside 'It's Bolt; I'm telling him his play's no good,' then informing him, 'I've got *Simon Callow* here and I'm telling him your play's *no good*.' Whatever his response was, it made her chuckle richly. 'Well it isn't, dear, is it?' There were more calls, all rapidly despatched; to my astonishment, she seemed to think that talking to me and, even more surprising, listening to me, was more important than the day-to-day business of running the most successful play agency in the country, perhaps the world. She dismissed *that* in a phrase. 'The word *agent*,' she said, 'is the most disgusting word in the English language.'

Names flew about the room, resonant, legendary, as the conversation got under way. She was on, not first but – so much more intimate – *last*-name terms with them all: Lean, Ionesco, Miller; nor was she confined to the living, or those whom she might have known personally: Proust, Cocteau, Rilke, were all swept up in the torrent of allusion and anecdote. It was immediately evident that she judged her clients, and herself, by direct comparison with the great dead. This gave the conversation uncommon breadth; but it was the least of what made the meeting extraordinary.

The overwhelming impression was of the airy, fiery presence of the woman herself. She was never still, not for a second, but there was nothing restless about her. She seemed rather to be performing a *moto perpetuo*, choreographed by some innovative genius into the physical representation of a dancing mind. Her long-fingered hands fluttered, her hair flew out of control, her slight frame drew itself up and up as if she were preparing for a high dive, then would suddenly flop down till she was almost horizontal in her chair, arms stretched out, legs shockingly wide apart, nether regions barely concealed by whichever small part of her transparent skirt was theoretically supposed to be covering her. Sometimes, to make a point, she would reach for a book or a script, wrap her fist round the arm of her spectacles, then whisk them off, thrusting her face flush up against the page. When she'd read what it was she was looking for, she'd unceremoniously throw the book or script down and shove her spectacles back onto her face. Even this alarming procedure was somehow gracefully effected.

The incessancy of movement was complemented by a voice as beautiful and expressive as any actress might hope to possess: perfectly modulated, feathery light and caressing, then suddenly rough and emphatic, but never when you expected it. Harsh things were said beautifully, beautiful things harshly; four-letter words were deployed like jewels. 'I always thought,' she said, liltingly, 'how *touching* it was that when Ken and Joe couldn't find anyone else to fuck, they would fuck *each other*.' Her vowels bore the very slightest trace of her native South Africa, which added a touch of the exotic, more a colour than a sound.

Conversational life was made even more exciting with the appearance of an occasional hole in the fabric of her talk. A word would suddenly elude her, and she would search furiously for it. The oddity was that while hundreds of unerringly chosen words in several languages, evidence of the widest possible literary culture, would flow past with seamless elegance, there would be a sudden hiatus: 'so I put the book on the – the – what do you call that thing?' 'What thing, Peggy? What sort of thing?' 'You know perfectly well: the *thing* you use when you want to put other *things* on it.' 'Dumb waiter? Sideboard?' 'Ya cha-cha-cha,' she would cry, dismissively. 'Trolley, Peggy?' A look of withering contempt. And then, in desperation, one would say, 'Table?' 'Table. *Exactly*.' And we were off again. This could apply equally to proper names; again, hardly the ones you'd expect, after disquisitions on Jean-Jacques Bertrand and Montherlant, laced with citations of large slices of Franz Werfel, all perfectly attributed. 'I first met Schneider because he'd done the American première of *Waiting for Godot* and he wanted to meet . . . he wanted to meet . . . ' (triumphantly) '*whoever it was that wrote it.*'

She had a characteristic method of phrasing which bore some resemblance to Queen Victoria's epistolary manner. Words were swooped on and singled out for special attention. Her style was essentially musical: a long legato line in the main body of the sentence, and then the crucial words drawn out in a deeper tone, accompanied by noddings of the head and downward floating motions of the hands: 'the important thing in life is to do whatever you want but then . . . *always* . . . *to pick up* . . . THE BILL.' The phrase would then hang in the air for silent moments while you both contemplated its majestic truthfulness.

7

Life, and its handmaiden, Art, were her topics, even on this first impromptu meeting. She fiercely announced their paradoxical twin demands: on the one hand, discipline, industry, and solitude; on the other, a life lived to the hilt, mentally, physically, above all emotionally. Between these two poles, in either art or life, there was, as far as she was concerned, nothing whatever of the slightest value. Marriage, friendship, parties, pastimes: all fruitless and destructive, she insisted. Independence, from people or from things, was the essential: 'expect nothing, and *everything* becomes a *bonus*.' Whereupon, ever-surprising, she suddenly informed me, having discovered that I had had my start in the theatre in the Box Office, 'of course, the Box Office is the only truly *romantic* part of the theatre.' And she meant it: she described the excitement of doing a deal, the thrill of watching the money come in; she had, she told me, a kind of Midas touch, and loved playing the Stock Exchange, for which she showed some talent. Clearly though, this was a holiday from the serious business of reminding authors of their sacred obligations, to Art and to Life.

Every word that came out of her mouth that day was completely unexpected, as unforeseen as our meeting. My jaw hung open most of the time, when, that is, I wasn't roaring with laughter, or suddenly moved almost to tears to find someone who spoke so unashamedly and with such hard-edged unsentimental eloquence about art, its power and its demands. It was my own view entirely, as was her view of life itself. Agony or ecstasy, I, at the age of 30, thought, and to hell with the bits in between; and so did she at what I later discovered to be 70, though the evidence of my eyes would have rejected that figure, had I been told it, as preposterous. At this first meeting we spurred each other on higher and higher with great thoughts and terrible truths until we finally fell silent, having completely exhausted ourselves. I got up to go and we shook hands, oddly, awkwardly. She sat at her desk, combing her hair and repairing her lipstick as I left the office. Going back through the reception area to pick up the script which I dimly remembered had been the occasion of my being there at all, I caught the eyes of the secretaries and blushed. It was as if Peggy and I had been making love.

2

As I walked away from the office, dazed and exhilarated, back down the perilous staircase, past the announcements of Bond in Oslo and Hare in Bochum, I laughed out loud at the improbability of what had just happened. My eagerness to avoid meeting her when I had first entered the office had been founded on a long-distance brush we'd had some years before, an incident she seemed now, to my great relief, to have totally forgotten. The play I had collected that day was Martin Sherman's *Passing By*, and it was another play by the same author, *Bent*, which had been the cause of the incident. I had been a play-reader for the Royal Court Theatre at the time; Max Stafford-Clark, then running the place, had asked if I had read any new plays I thought worth doing. I recommended *Bent*, which Martin had shown me as soon as he had written it. Max wanted to see a copy; Peggy's office apparently had none. Martin being out the country at the time, I helpfully taxied at top speed what appeared to be the only copy of the play in London from Shepherd's Bush, where it was, to the theatre in Sloane Square.

The moment this coup of mine was reported to Peggy, she let off a broadside to Martin of such vigour that he and I were both stunned into silence, an extraordinarily fierce display of professional territorialism on the part of the woman who had just told me that *agent* was the most disgusting world in the English language. '*Some actor,*' she wired him, 'is interfering with the agency's work. Stop him immediately, or consider yourself unrepresented.' At Martin's understandably urgent request, I desisted. The play was put on some while later (at the Royal Court Theatre, in fact, as it happens) to enormous acclaim, but the incident had given me a healthy respect for her formidable fire-breathing authority, even at long distance.

This fierce exchange had not prepared me in the least for my recent encounter at Goodwin's Court. This was no Wagnerian dragon, far from it. Beauty, fire, passion, sex, brilliance, elegance, charm and a sort of impersonal, ego-less force of character, were the qualities that came to mind. Her sheer animation, coupled with the lightest, most graceful of touches, was the single most striking impression, hard to convey except by extravagant simile: a fire-breathing butterfly? A cross between a dolphin and a humming-bird? I felt as if I had met a great figure of the past, a Mme de Sévigné or a Harriet Martineau. Not that there was any-thing old-fashioned about Peggy, unless you counted her unbreakable conviction that nothing was more important or more powerful than art. In every regard, she seemed years younger than I in her tastes and fascinations.

There was no denying that she was eccentric. Reporting that first encounter, I amused myself, and others, by saying that Peggy had behaved like a madwoman suffering from the delusion that she was the greatest play agent in the world.

What I actually thought was that I'd met someone touched by genius.

I found out everything that I could about her, which was not a great deal; most of it was contradictory. There were stories without punch-lines, vague rumours of liaisons with Ionesco, with Adamov, with Beckett; someone thought she'd once been an actress, someone else that she'd been a singer. There was a story about her walking out on her husband the moment he and she arrived in London from South Africa. Her age was shrouded in mystery; Christopher Hampton claimed that a secretary who had accidentally found it out when entrusted with her passport had shortly after drowned in mysterious circumstances, taking her secret with her to a watery grave. What was not in doubt was her unique contribution to the British Theatre: she seemed to represent every living playwright of any importance except, I noted with curiosity, those whose names ended in -er: Shaffer, Pinter, Wesker. On examination, in fact, there were plenty of distinguished writers whom she didn't represent (Stoppard, Bennett and Osborne among them); but every agent in London acknowledged her as their doyenne and a model of what an agent might be: putting lead into her writers' pencils and iron into their souls, money in their purses and sometimes roofs over their heads; giving courage to timid producers and advice to uncertain directors. She had, above all, a positively papal reputation for being *right*. It was very daunting and deeply intriguing.

Shortly after our meeting at Goodwin's Court, I received a letter from her, the first of many in an unbroken flow that only stopped with her death some eleven years later. In this first, almost formal, letter she suggested a play that she thought might interest me, a French piece in which a pig addresses the audience at some length before being taken to the abattoir. It was the first occasion that Peggy attempted to do something for me, also the first of many, many such attempts. I was still playing at the National Theatre in repertory, in *Amadeus*, *As You Like It*, *Galileo* (translated by Peggy's client Howard Brenton) and *Sisterly Feelings* (by

Peggy's client Alan Ayckbourn), and I was beginning to do a series of pre-show Platform Performances in which I introduced and performed Shakespeare's Sonnets in a new sequence devised by Dr John Padel, building up to the extraordinary occasion one summer's afternoon when I would perform all 154 in the Olivier auditorium. I was at the theatre day and night.

One evening quite soon after my first meeting with Peggy I arrived at the theatre to find the stage door staff in a state of some excitement: a crate of vintage wines from Fortnum and Mason had been delivered, simply labelled 'National Theatre Stage Door'. No one knew who it was for or from whom it had come. In the absence of a legitimate claimant, the stage door keepers were already in their mind's eyes knocking it back themselves; eventually, to their chagrin, the National's press department placed a piece about the phantom plonk in the Londoner's Diary of the Evening Standard. The next day Peggy Ramsay's office called the National with the information that it was she who had sent it, and that the intended recipient was me. I phoned to thank her. She was amazed that neither I nor anyone else had realised that the wine was for me. She had, she said, been walking down Piccadilly, musing on the fact that it was Molière's birthday and that not a single actor in England would know, much less care. Musing on this sad reality, it had suddenly struck her that, yes, there was an actor in England who would know and care: me. And so she had gone into Fortnum's and ordered the wine and had it sent to me, to celebrate, with my actor friends, the great playwright's birthday. I could hardly admit that my ignorance of the anniversary was quite as great as, if not greater than, that of every other actor in England, so instead I spoke passionately about Molière and his work (this at least was not a fraud) and suggested, *en passant*, that she might like to attend a performance of the Shakespeare Sonnets the following week.

The letter she sent me after that performance was quite different from the first one she had written me, quite unlike any letter anyone had ever written me. She had written to Peter Hall, she told me, telling him that I was his rose and that he must look after me. 'In case you don't know the St Exupéry book *Le Petit Prince*,' she wrote, 'the little Prince finds a rose and tends it, and defends it from the wind, and from other dangers, but he complains that it's a strain, and that, after all, *his* rose is only one of many roses. The story-teller then speaks very firmly to the little Prince and says that *because* he has cared for it and protected it, *it is his rose*, and not like any other, and that it is *because* he has taken so much trouble that the rose is so important, and that he is therefore *responsible* for it.' Then she added: 'It's really all about love,' and continued, characteristically, but inaccurately, 'Exupéry was a homosexual, and had, I suppose, these hidden passions for the 'forbidden' . . . he is talking about the *responsibility* of loving, even if it is unrequited.' Somewhat unexpectedly she added: 'It is appropriate to the 'pure' feeling P Hall has for you and I'm telling him he is *responsible* for you!' She promised to send me a recording Gérard Philippe had made of *Le Petit Prince*, and finally signed off, 'The understanding and passion of your performance was an overwhelming experience. One began by *listening* to the sonnets, and then one *became part of Shakespeare* in the greatest depths. Yours Peggy R'. A day later she wrote to me 'If you've now read the English *Petit Prince* (the tape is being made for you), didn't you love the Fox saying that the PP should warn him when he was coming "so that he could prepare his heart".' Then she added, 'This reminds me of Ionesco, whose wife didn't like him spending much time in my company. After we'd spent an afternoon together and he was preparing to face the dreaded Rosica he turned to me anxiously and said, "Are my eyes too bright?"– "est-ce que mes yeux *brillent* trop?"'

This letter came accompanied by three pages of hand-written quotations, of which the most striking was a passage from Maupassant: 'We must feel, that is everything. We must feel as a brute beast, filled with nerves, feels, and knows that it has felt, and knows that each feeling shakes it like an earthquake. But we must not say that we have been so shaken. At the most, we can let it be known to a few people who will respect the confidence.' Almost equally arresting was another quotation, from Gertrude Stein: 'It is inevitable that when one has great need of something one finds it. What you need you attract like a lover.' Peggy's next letter, a day later, equally full of intense expression, ended 'Yesterday's Shakespeare reading scorched me like a forest fire, and I am finding it hard to recover.'

'Dear, dear, dear Simon,' her next letter began, 'you have a temperament which vibrates at the fall of a leaf and I seriously question if we should continue to correspond in case we disturb one another. The trouble is that your performance if anything throws out a *secret*. But what the secret is, one does not know: (This secret whispered to an audience is the mark of the great actor.) I have a kind of ESP and catch reverberations which are not usually heard (like a dog catches notes too high for the human ear). Also my Slav blood compels me to write letters one ought NOT to (like Tatiana in *Onegin*) and I should know better.' Astonished and humbled, I realised that the extraordinary woman I was

15

coming to know had experienced a *coup de foudre*. She had fallen in love with me, completely and instantaneously. Life was imitating art; the Sonnets, after all, are precisely about being taken over by an overpowering love for someone who remains essentially unknown. While I was working on them I had been in the throes of just such an emotion myself, and had been shaken to the core by my work on them. In rehearsal I had sometimes been unable to continue without breaking down. Even in performance, I would sometimes be overwhelmed by waves of feeling which perhaps distorted the meaning of the poems but which, I was convinced, were somehow true to the poet's experience. It was this, I had no doubt, this personal engagement of mine with the experience behind the poems, which had unerringly communicated itself to Peggy.

It was because of the relationship that had so devastated me during my work on the Sonnets that I knew with such certainty what had happened. It had happened to me more than once in my life, the love which suddenly arrives, like a god in a chariot, but for once, this time, when I had fallen passionately in love with a young Turkish-Egyptian film-maker, exquisitely graceful and mysteriously elusive, called Aziz Yehia, he had, by what seemed to me the most miraculous good fortune, fallen in love with me, too.

He was an exquisite individual in many ways, perfect in his manners, acquired in the best Swiss schools and on the international circuit of the dispossessed Turkish and Egyptian haute bourgeoisie, beautiful to behold, bearing more than a passing resemblance to the young Alain Delon, slight, olive-skinned, brown-eyed and long-lashed, seductive in a feminine but not in the least effeminate way. He was also brilliantly eloquent in the manner of the brightest products of the French educational system: full of paradox, allusion and witty analysis, by turn sententious, semiotic and structuralist, volubly quoting Lacan, Derrida, Lévi-Strauss. In all of these ways, he left me far behind; I thought him a bit of a genius. He was also, as I was just beginning properly to understand, frighteningly aware of a dark emptiness at his centre, a void, a block, a paralysis of the soul, which drove him across ever-wider extremes of emotional experience in search of a sense of personal reality that grew more and more elusive. Highs got higher and lows got lower, until what seemed at first like a perfectly normal oscillation of spirits was unmistakably, even to a layman, and an infatuated one at that, manic depression. Even now, fairly close to the beginning of our time together, there were unexpected losses of centre, as if he had suddenly forfeited all sense of the parameters of his personality. There would be terrible conversational misjudgements, even physical solecisms, a hand too intimately applied, or too roughly. Under the influence of his preferred tipple, the fiercely strong Carlsberg Special Brew lager (he had no taste for wine or spirits), he could become quite vulgar or silly beyond belief, in curious contrast to the charm of his person, the polish of his manners, and the sophistication of his wit. I saw but dismissed these occasional and brief aberrations. To know him was to enter what was for me a strange and thrilling new universe, different from anything I had ever known. It was meat and drink, it was opera and it was a three-volume novel. I could scarcely believe that it was happening to me.

Our relationship had been going on for three over-whelming months when I met Peggy. I wanted to come clean about it straight away, but first she and I had to meet again, and take stock of our new relationship. Things had been moving forward between us with alarming speed. We were already becoming prolific correspondents, and now began to have epic telephone conversations, generally during the long hours when I was sitting in my dressing room between my scenes in *Galileo*. I became more and more fascinated by the beauty of her voice, and one day I told her so. The remark stopped her dead. I knew that my simple compliment had pierced her to the core. For the most part, we talked of plays, exhibitions, concerts. She was a great purveyor of high level literary gossip, much of it concerning the dead. During one of these conversations, I suggested casually that it would be nice to have supper one evening. She offered to cook for me; I accepted, eagerly.

Some time the following week, late on a balmy May night, I went on to her place after my show, and rang the bell of the basement flat in Redcliffe Square with a nervousness which mingled excitement and anxiety. I wanted to know everything I could about this remarkable woman. I had always had a rapport with women of a certain age (my grandmothers had been powerful and formative figures in my childhood), but with Peggy I felt a directness of communication that was different from any such relationship in the past, or maybe from any relationship at all. It was almost frighteningly intimate, frighteningly soon. The difference in our circumstances – our ages, our positions in the world – seemed not to matter at all, but I had no model, no framework for what was developing so quickly between us. Evidently there was no question, with this woman, of holding back; it must be all or nothing. There could be no choice but to let it happen: let the dice fall where they may. I rang again; eventually the door opened.

I hope Peggy didn't hear my gasp. She had transformed herself into a young woman, her hair newly coiffed, her silk housecoat fluttering about her. Underneath was very little indeed, only a slip through which the outline of her shapely breasts was plainly visible. On it she had pinned an exotic flower, a gardenia or perhaps an orchid. The smell of this flower enveloped us both as I stooped to peck her cheek. When I did, she started to shake. She tore herself away, talking torrentially, babbling almost, asking questions but not waiting for replies, wafting me down the hall, which, like most of the rest of the flat, was plunged in darkness apart from a few strategically-placed candles, one of which she swept up to light the way. She was describing the flat, waving and gesturing with her candle-hand, hot wax flying in all directions. She had no shoes on, nor was she wearing her spectacles, which led to occasional collisions with furniture, but, bobbing and ducking and weaving, she managed to gather up quantities of food – chicken, ham, pâté, cheese, salad, dressing, snatching up bottles of wine as she went – and steered us into the garden. This was a vision in itself. With a hundred candles in small jars placed across the flowerbeds, she had transformed what I took to be a small nondescript space into a shimmering grotto. She produced blankets and we sat down for our midnight picnic. She was an anxious hostess, apologising for the food, the blankets, the garden. I told her that she looked beautiful. So she did, trembling with life and emotion, everything fluttering: hands, gown, heart. My praise again pierced her, seemed almost to hurt her, to give her physical pain. She took breaths in great gusts. I don't know what we spoke about; nothing much, I think; the great conversations came later. Here, on this summer night, I was simply astonished to be sitting in this chimerical grotto, with this fragile, exotic creature fuelled by a sort of helium compounded of emotion and strong physical need.

A black cat suddenly appeared from on high, and sauntered over to partake of a little light collation. Peggy addressed it in cat language: 'Come-eelong, come-eelong, wah wah wah. This is Button,' she told me, 'the little Button. I used to think that Button was a man. But he's not. He's a woman. When I found out that he was a woman, I felt filled with pity for her.'

The evening went on into the small hours. I could see no need for it to end at all, but finally, out of convention, took my leave. When I kissed her good-night, she shook again, and then let out a tremendous sigh. Almost pushing me out of the flat, she shut the door abruptly. I had the impression, as I walked home, that she felt that she had made a fool of herself. She hadn't. She had simply presented herself in the most vulnerable way she possibly could have done. Gone was the scourge of lazy writers, gone the searching editor, gone the power-broker, gone the celebrated lover. In their place was a young belle on her first serious assignation, or Tatiana, as she herself had suggested in her letter, receiving Onegin. I only admired her the more for that, loved her for it, in fact. I knew then that I loved her. I did not desire her, as she must have known. I suspect that this al fresco evening had been in some way an unconscious attempt at seduction, regardless of the impossibility of the situation. Though our love grew stronger and stronger, she never ever attempted anything like it again. This evening was, I believe, a farewell to seduction for her, she who must have been the most potent seducer imaginable.

I had also failed to tell her about Aziz.

3

That night, as we sat having our little *souper sur l'herbe*, Peggy's client David Mercer died in Israel, of a heart attack. His death winded her for a moment, though she thought it was all for the best. He was finished as a writer, she said, neutrally; what else was there to live for? She later told me about the tribute to him performed at the Aldwych Theatre, and how upset everybody had been. She thought that a wholly inappropriate response, although she took time to console David Warner, one of Mercer's best interpreters. 'Poor little Warner,' she said. 'He was distracted with grief. It took me ten minutes to calm him up.' Calming up would be Peggy's way.

We continued to correspond, on an almost daily basis, and she became franker in her expression of her feelings. 'May I touch on my feeling for you? It's the opposite of Aschenbach, who saw Tadziu as the bearer of death. I see you coming quickly into a room (or onto a stage), your hair is blowing outward, and you are talking and laughing and I am choked with emotion, because what is coming towards me is LIFE.' In my letters to her, I took it head on; there could be no other way. 'I'm overwhelmed to think that someone like you can feel that about me,' I wrote to her. 'Thank you. I do so passionately believe that the only meaning of life is life, that to live is the deepest obligation we have, and that to help other people live is the greatest achievement. It's in that light that I see acting, and that alone.' Then I told her about Aziz.

'What you say about love,' I wrote to her, 'is EXACTLY what I believe. Loving is so much more important than being loved. I only recently understood this, realised that this was my greatest need. I allowed myself to love someone for the first time in four years (as opposed I mean to sexing, which is so easy and so unmemorable) and although he doesn't love me the way I love him, he *allows* me to love him with such grace and good will that I don't mind in the least that it's not really reciprocated. (I do him an injustice – it is reciprocated, in so far as he can. He has no gift for loving – his gift is for being loved.) As for my feelings for you: I am thrilled that you've entered my life. Your vitality and nurturing passion ring such loud bells with me, I feel an extraordinary sense of sympathy between us, and hope to God that we can sustain that most beautiful and elusive thing, a passionate friendship . . . '

I did not then attempt to describe Aziz to her; I simply registered the depth of my feeling for him. He and I had met some two and a half years before. He had then been involved with a mutual friend, but in the fullness of time, this involvement had come to an end, and I had seized my moment. To my amazement, we had become lovers on our first date and had pursued our romance with increasing fervour. I had been enchanted by him on first sight, captivated by the dark glamour of his looks, dazzled by his conversation, elated by his exotic background. Half-Turkish and half-Egyptian, born in Alexandria, he had escaped with his family to Switzerland at the time of Nasser's coup. He had graduated brilliantly from the University of Geneva and then, having made a witty, stylish short film on Super-

8, he applied to the National Film School in Beaconsfield, and they had accepted him. He had been studying there for the last four years, and had made two very elegant short films for them, one rather Hitchcockian, the other a little Marivaux-like anecdote. He was brilliantly witty in four languages, bewilderingly fluent in structuralist analysis, profoundly immersed in celluloid, and tortured by his relationship with his mother, about whom he spoke freely and amusingly, but with an underlying rage which was almost disturbing. 'My mother,' he would say, 'wears my balls on a brooch.' I personally was unaware of any absence of balls, but it was nonetheless clear that behind the brilliance, the grace and the vulnerability were some overmastering emotions which made it almost impossible for him to give wholly and freely of himself, however caring and playful he might be. He was sexual but not passionate, loving but not in love. To that extent, our relationship was not without its frustrations, for me at any rate, but it was still the most extraordinary emotional experience of my life so far. Something un-English, un-European, even, in him had had a profoundly liberating effect on me, physically, mentally, emotionally. Frozen oceans within me had melted, and I was often unable to deal with the attendant floods, which sometimes threatened to engulf me. I was a changed man. The very speed of my commitment to Peggy, in fact, would not have been possible without what I had experienced with Aziz.

I did not attempt to convey even a tenth of this when I wrote to her about him. I did nothing but state the bald facts. She replied breezily to my letter. Of course she knew about Aziz, she said – he had been spotted: 'At the first night of the Brecht a lovely young man was pointed out to me as your rose by Tom (who knows everything) and I hoped then that you were happy and that you loved him.' Nothing was changed, as far as she was concerned; if I could live with it, she said, so would she. She didn't ask whether Aziz could live with it; nor did I. He was fascinated by what I told him about her, but deeply involved in post-producing his last film at Beaconsfield, working round the clock. Peggy and I were therefore free to pursue our friendship, which we did, at lightning speed. 'Simon!!!! Your letter dated 14th arrived today 26th! And what a *lovely* letter! I'd been thinking (till I got it) that I am somehow intruding on your life and that it was rather boring for you, or embarrassing. Yes, I would love to be your passionate friend, but I don't know anything about friendship. I've always found my friendships in books and art. Sex and gambling were my passions, but of course the people (I suppose!) one remembers are the ones one didn't have. This perhaps is why I don't quite know how to behave properly with you. But I will try; provided I can be a bit wild, now and again. If you *knew* how I wish I were a slim, dark young man you fancied! How blissful that would be. And that wretched Egyptian doesn't know how fantastically lucky he is . . . '

So that was all right, then. I began writing to Peggy, and talking to her, about what I was going through with Aziz. 'I want commitment, and burning passion and reckless gestures: and what I have instead is beauty and grace and irony and tenderness and sympathy and wit. I love him Peggy; what I'm raging about is simply the OTHERNESS of the other person, the source of all love's pain.' I was deliberately exposing her to the reality of the depths of my feelings for Aziz, trying to judge it as carefully as I could to spare her pain. I failed. 'Our friendship has cost me

24

quite a bit of anguish,' she wrote to me, 'which is why I so *completely* understand what you are going through. People are coming in (and there have been half a dozen L.A. calls) all saying how gay and chipper I seem (*wild*, I'd call it) and they little know! But *ich grolle nicht* (I do not complain). I, too, will hold on to my dark pride! And you are so completely delicious that what's a slight ache? Sweet, sweet, sweet, puppy, puppy, puppy.' It was now that I became 'the puppy,' which I remained right to the end, 'the little puppy.' My canine traits were cited sometimes admiringly, often critically, but always, in the last analysis, forgivingly.

Peggy and I started to meet regularly, for lunches mostly, at Pizzaland in Covent Garden, a suitably neutral rendez-vous, neither of us daring to risk a repetition of the al fresco supper in Redcliffe Square. Our friendship was clearly destined to be. Both of us wanted it. For whatever reason, we had been placed in each other's path; there was no way of escaping it. I had no desire to escape it. Love had always been the supreme imperative to me; when it called, I abandoned everything, and this was love, unmistakably. Our relationship was already complex, and getting deeper, and more complex, every day. The fact that the love was between a seventy year-old woman and a thirty year-old gay man ('queer,' as Peggy always put it, caressing the word) and was never going to be consummated physically complicated matters, certainly, but it did nothing to invalidate it. The difference in our feelings for each other was in kind, not in intensity. I was fascinated by her, obsessed by her, in fact. I could scarcely talk of anyone else when I was with my friends. I was fascinated, too, almost hypnotised, by the scale of her feelings. Perhaps, it occurred to me, somewhat wryly, what I felt for Peggy was not unlike what Aziz felt for me: intrigued, touched, thrilled, even, by the love provoked, without being quite able to replicate it. It was I who made all the running, at this moment in my relationship with Aziz, I who was the supplicant, I who suffered; whereas in my friendship with Peggy, I was the recipient, I accepted her love, and gave back mine as best I could. This we all acknowledged, all three of us. The crucial difference, of course, was that Aziz and I had the blissful relief of physical consummation; with Peggy there was none. This curious triangular situation was part of our lives from the beginning; it never really resolved itself.

Never having met him, Peggy became almost as involved in Aziz as I was, devoting hours and hours of her time to an analysis of what she called his problem: namely, his failure to love me as much as I loved him, or indeed as much as she loved me. In fact, of course, he was really *her* problem – his very existence in my life, that is. She resented his hold over me; but equally, she deplored his refusal to give me what I gave him, even though if he did, we would surely give ourselves up to each other so completely that there would then be no room for anyone else in my heart; no room for Peggy. In fact, though, she doubted whether the thing I most believed in, the idea of an absolute union between two people, was either possible or desirable. 'I'm not sure that two people should become one, if one loves. You wrote of the 'otherness' of the object of your desire. But you cannot make the loved one *you*. Nor should you wish it. Perhaps you should *rejoice* that there are things within you that are *not* shared or understood – a sort of pride? A feeling that your passion transcends? Those of us whose nature drives us should regret *nothing* – life should be torn apart, ripped open, savaged,' she wrote. 'It doesn't matter if one makes a fool of oneself, becomes a spectacle. One *is*; one is *alive*.' Then she came to what was for her the nub of the whole thing: 'This can be poured into your work, which is more important than any single individual, *however* desirable or wonderful! It is the whole mainspring of art; the *impossibility* of becoming 'one' with any living soul, because you are one of life's delicate children, an artist, and it is the fate of the artist to love those whose grace and beauty allow them to fit easily into the world, by virtue of their charm, their wit – they are there, *the loved*, and that is enough. You must reserve your dark pride. I send you love, love, love.'

Implicit was her belief that she and I were kindred, and that Aziz was not of our number. Nonetheless, if I loved him, she would do everything she could to smooth our way. 'We have so much going between us that I am *altogether* happy to have your friendship, and accept with vicarious pleasure that you love someone physically, but I feel *frantic* when I think he cannot and will not give you all the wonderful violent things that two people should give one another, and I really feel unbearably upset that you should be deprived of anything. And when you said, 'Nothing is perfect,' I could have wept. Between two people who care sexually about one another, yes it *must* be perfect, even if it doesn't last forever. Well, there's Venice, and then he is here for a week – perhaps it WILL be perfect for you – it has GOT to be. THIS IS AN INDISCREET LETTER. BUT AREN'T *ALL* MY LETTERS TO YOU (one way or another).'

Now that his time at Film School had come to an end, Aziz and I planned to spend a fortnight in Venice, but he had meanwhile returned to Switzerland, to sort out his affairs and to decide what to do with his life. He had graduated with distinction from Beaconsfield, but it was far from clear to him how to take the next step and actually become a film-maker, a 'real film-maker,' as he used to say. He had been in full-time education all his conscious life, and was now, at the age of thirty, faced with a very cold dose of reality. He had no financial problems; his mother was still living on the jewels (Romanoff) that they had brought out with them from Alexandria, where Aziz's father had been an immensely wealthy businessman. But this lack of financial pressure made things worse, of course. He didn't have to do anything, if he didn't want to. He did want to, insofar as he had any conception of what working for his living might actually be like; like Baron Tusenbach in *Three Sisters*, he used to speak most movingly of the beauty and sanctity of work. He had rather enjoyed serving as a grip or a gaffer on his contemporaries' films at Beaconsfield, but he simply couldn't seem to take the steps required to get a job. Also he felt sure that the problems that he had with his mother needed to be addressed as a matter of urgency, and so he applied himself to the question of selecting an analyst, which he finally did, settling on an English Jungian who practised in Zurich. He had told his mother about me – not, I think, actually spelling out the nature of our relationship; his homosexuality had been acknowledged but was never alluded to except as the subject of bitter reproaches during the frequent stormy outbursts which characterised their relationship – and she had impulsively invited me to come for a weekend, arranging a ticket to Geneva for me.

Thus began my intimate knowledge of the airports of Europe. The weekend was a triumph; Aziz's mother and I got on famously, but I saw instantly and with deep fore-boding what an all-consuming phenomenon their emotion for each other was, the relationship more that of lovers than of mother and son. I came back to England confused but more fascinated than ever by the exotic complexities of both his background and his psyche; fuller than ever of longing for him, a longing only intensified by our geographical separation and by my dim awareness that a large part of him was forever engaged in a no-holds-barred fight with his mother for his very survival.

Peggy was full of advice and encouragement, and urged me to follow my heart, whatever the cost, emotionally or financially. This meant heading for Geneva at every possible opportunity, which I gladly did, thanks to the accommo-dating schedule of the National Theatre. As I flew to meet Aziz on one such occasion, on a ticket that this time Peggy had insisted on paying for (life had now become very complicated indeed), I wrote her a letter: 'On the plane to Geneva and high as a kite: or, in fact, of course, much higher. I must thank you again for your impossible generosity. I wonder if you know what it's like to be showered with unstinting and unearned gifts? Not much, I guess; because you're so obviously a giver rather than given to; but so am I, and I can tell you it feels wonderful. It's to be a child again, to feel that simply because of who you are, you deserve reward.' In truth, like all good lower-middle-class boys and girls, I felt profoundly uneasy about being given money without having earned it. I tried to justify it to my-self, and in doing so stumbled on a truth. 'Partly I accept,' I wrote, 'because it is true, as you say, that if I had the money and you needed it I would give it to you. But actu-ally it's not a question of needing. I don't need it. That's the truly marvellous part of it all. To give to people who need it is noble; but to give to those that don't – that is divine. So thank you and thank you again. I don't think I ever felt so *rewarded* – no, no, that's not it, I feel rewarded by a good notice or a good salary: for something I've done. With you I feel that it's for something I am: you make me feel worthy of love; and not many people have done that.' I signed the letter as the plane touched down at Geneva Airport.

It was obvious that sooner or later the three of us must meet; it was, as Peggy said, the *scène à faire*, the 'obligatory scene' of nineteenth-century dramaturgy. I quickly understood that one of the reasons that Peggy had such a keen sense of the way in which plays worked – or didn't – was that her view of life was fundamentally dramatic. She dramatised everything, made everything dramatic. The idea of Aziz would sometimes inflame Peggy to fever pitch. She longed to meet him, and dreaded it. 'I want Aziz and I (me?) to meet on a blind date first. I don't think I can meet the two of you *together* the first time. I'm therefore enclosing a very boring snap, which he can see and then tear up please. And may I have a snap of Aziz? So we can know roughly who and accost!' She more than half expected that once the meeting had taken place, she would have to acknowledge the superior force of our love, his and mine, and that she would have to bow out. 'These are the last letters we shall write one another before Venice and perhaps the last of summer. Thank you darling Simon for all the happiness you have given me. You have guided our friendship marvellously – there is a feminine delicacy in you and an exquisite grace which Aziz evokes. How *wonderful* nature is to provide this ecstasy to be given and received by two people.'

We went to Venice, where Aziz shot a film whose plot he improvised on the spur of the moment, concerning the encounter between a slightly moody Englishman and an exotic stranger. It had a haunted, lonely feel to it, but it ended happily, to my relief. There were shadows between us, in this city of shadows, mainly to do with Aziz's uncertainty about his future; I saw for the first time that he was frightened for it, or rather frightened *of* it. This astonished me. I had been frustrated in the past by obstacles I saw on my path, but had never doubted that there was a path ahead, and that it lead to a destination, to many and varied destinations, in fact. For him, this was simply not true. We'd sit at Florian's and talk about what lay ahead, separately and together, and he'd smile distantly, indulging what he clearly saw as my charming fantasies. These moments passed, though, and we gave ourselves over to Venice, which he knew intimately. It was my first encounter with it, and I reported on it to Peggy, somewhat uncertainly flexing my literary muscles. 'We arrived by vaporetto, we ate wonderful meals, we drank coffee in squares, we wandered mapless at midnight over bridges and down alleys always surrounded by water, the same water, and seemingly the same buildings, forever passing by the same church, a dream landscape, utterly foreign but wholly familiar, lost but safe. We fell into melancholy, we gave up gasping at aquatic vistas. We never got hold of Venice; it was an invention of our own minds, not an external reality. Weather changed: the sky blackened and lightning flashed; seagulls wheeled crazily; bars of gold pierced the evening; reds and pinks painted the basilicas, the palazzi, the campi: and every change remade the city. It's obvious but inescapable to point out that it's theatre, the whole place:

insubstantial, brilliant, slightly vulgar, effects contrived not to be majestic, or beautiful or symmetrical but simply to be striking – to be effective. Enough,' I hastily ended, 'of purple p.'

By now our correspondence was in full flood. I was living out my entire life for her in letters, acutely conscious, and thus unhealthily self-conscious, that the recipient was one of the supreme judges of writing in our time. I wrote in many voices, not so much to gain her approval as to avoid her disapproval, which was notoriously fierce; I made stab after stab at a tone which was intended to be intimate and sophisticated and playful, and time after time I fell flat on my literary face. She never minded, never even commented. Her letters to me continued on a wave of molten lava, written for no reason except to communicate what was in her heart. 'It's wonderful for you to let me write to you as I do. The authors I look after are utterly *detached* from me, not friends. I've given a huge interview (I hope to Christ it will be anonymous) about the necessity of taking NOTHING from their kind of work. No credits no friendship no consolation!!! Perhaps your beautiful talent, which is as an actor, plus the extraordinary gift you have for writing, has allowed me to feel for you.' She concealed nothing; nor did I, but what I wrote was, at least to begin with, wrapped up in poses of one sort or another. She, on the other hand, was her style.

At the end of Venice, Aziz went back to Geneva, and I returned to England, and we too corresponded, huge long screeds, wildly romantic and silly, generally despatched express. The Post Office must have had a bonanza that year.

4

The vaunted meeting *à deux* between Peggy and Aziz continued to be unendingly discussed. 'I thought Aziz and I could lunch at a gallery,' wrote Peggy, 'or on a bench by the Thames – just a short encounter. (Why do I think this? I want to talk to a stranger, who happens to be Aziz.) But some other idea will do equally well.' Aziz then wrote her a letter, which expresses some of his coy cheekiness, but which, alas, could not have been worse judged in terms of its recipient or the situation.

'Genève le 16 Octobre 1980, Chère mademoiselle Peggy, I hope you will find the unforgivable lateness of this letter slightly less unforgivable if I explain that I wanted it to be "just so", and, as we all know, the desire for perfection is often an excuse for putting things off whilst waiting for that silly old lying bitch usually referred to as "inspiration". Well, mademoiselle, I am not "inspired", but I will ignore that fact and get on with the pleasurable business of epistolary communication with a lady I can't wait to meet next week – alone at first, as you delightfully suggested – and then with that charming young actor for whom we both seem to share some degree of affection, admiration and – oh let's be devils: LOVE. My unerring intuition leads me to anticipate that that puzzling emotion will be the main theme of our conversation(s) – your love for Simon, his for you, his for me, yours for us, mine for him, mine for . . . oh dear, you see, I'm getting carried away already, I who meant to be so suavely articulate. Oh well, never mind, a bit of artistic temperament doesn't hurt, now and then. What else shall we discuss? Beauty of course, with a capital B, no that's not enough: two capital B's, at least – and Art, too, that would be nice – and not the weather unless there's a hurricane or a flood . . . I do wonder what you're like, how close you are in the flesh to the image provided in part by Monsieur Callow, and in part by my feverish imagination. I know you're beautiful, from the snapshot (this is pure flattery BUT . . . I only flatter with the truth) also something of a Brain and a Wit and a Poet(ess) and a Dynamo with whom people have trouble catching up.

As for me, I am like this letter – brittle but vibrant, I like to think. But also cripplingly shy which, combined with an over-eagerness to please, can be fairly tiring. Ah, how silly to "plan" encounters, let's just see, shall we? En attendant je vous embrasse très fort (il paraît que vous n'aimez pas ça, mais tant pis) et je brûle d'impatience. I'm sure you speak perfect French but in case you don't, what I just wrote was: see you, Peggy. Yours sincerely Aziz.'

Peggy was baffled by this letter; she couldn't make him out at all. Nonetheless, shortly after, when Aziz was on a brief stay in England to see friends, the dreaded meeting finally took place, not after all à deux, which proved too alarming to both of them, but à trois.

This event, on which so many hopes and fears were predicated, turned out almost comic in the event – would actually have been so, in fact, had Peggy herself not been in such palpable distress. Aziz, for his part, was desperate, too, equally aware, from his side of the triangle, that he and I were not alone in this relationship, and that a large part of my mind and heart were now filled with the extraordinary being he was now meeting. For my part, I deeply wanted them to like each other, of course. The difference was that I couldn't see how each could fail to see in the other what I did; the moment they met, all imagined problems would surely dissolve. I even felt that perhaps these two remarkable people would realise that I was in fact rather less remarkable than either of them, that they would go off into the sunset together leaving me with nothing but a dazzling memory. Of course I didn't dare to entertain this as a serious possibility, but the build-up to this occasion had been so long and so fraught that it had lost its reality. Anyway, here we finally were, each of us eagerly pursuing our separate objectives.

On this evening, the obligatory evening, both he and Peggy were as high as kites when we picked her up in a taxi at Redcliffe Square. Aziz wanted to impress Peggy intellectually, to charm her, to flirt with her, to be kind to her, and, most important, to let her know how deeply involved he and I were. Peggy was grimly determined that the evening should be fun. I found myself becoming almost monolithic in my desire to ground the evening in some kind of normality. We went (my eccentric choice) to a now defunct restaurant in Lots Road, Fulham, called *All My Eye and Betty Martin*. The larky name (an alleged mishearing by a British sailor of the phrase Ah mihi, Beati Martini) accurately expressed the strained larkiness of the menu and the service, which did nothing to calm things down. I had failed to check where the restaurant was, and accordingly we spent twenty minutes of increasing hysteria stumbling around in the dark and rather menacing streets trying to find it, with the great Power Station looming unhelpfully above us, Aziz in his best Savile Row suit and Peggy dressed as if for Royal Ascot. Things were more than a little strained when we finally got there. Aziz was shy at first; I was prefect-like, trying to organise the eating and drinking, in which neither of the other two seemed remotely interested, while Peggy talked energetically and indiscreetly about the business of the office that day, fascinating to me but drawing a bit of a blank from Aziz. I suppose she then thought it advisable to talk about someone of whom he might have heard. 'Last night I was going through some old papers at home, and I found a box full of Sam Beckett's letters,' she said, 'so I threw them away.' The shocked silence that followed this remark was profound and seemed to go through the whole of the restaurant. 'In a bin marked Sotheby's, I hope,' I remarked. 'What?' said Peggy. 'What do you mean?' I pointed out that they might be valuable. 'Not to me,' she said. 'I keep nothing, and nor should you,' she told me, 'and you must only have in your flat things that you love, little creature.' I said I would do my best. It was a great theme of hers, this, the importance of having nothing in your life but what is essential, and now she hammered it home with violent force. (I was always to disappoint her in this regard.) I sensed that Aziz was feeling redundant. Peggy was speaking to me with a kind of tender, demanding care that was of such intimacy that it made the rest of the room disappear. 'We will look after him, Miss Ramsay,' said Aziz, firmly, 'take care of all his needs.' 'You can take care of *all* his needs,' she said, 'I can't. Alas. It would be nice, but I am resigned.'

She fiercely quizzed Aziz on his life and his background, hearing about his mother with many tut-tuts, probing his hopes and aspirations as a film-maker and promising to introduce him to people in the industry who might help him. He in turn asked her about herself, but drew a complete blank. 'What do you want to know?' she said. 'There is nothing to know. I'm *not interesting*.' Finally, the meal at an end (she of course snatched up the bill: 'ya cha-cha cha-cha cha'), we repaired to my flat in Notting Hill Gate and sat on the sofa, drinking and talking (in fact, *I* was drinking and talking for three) while the Venetian harlequin we had bought her in one of the shops off the Grand Canal lolled, neglected, in a colourful stupor at her side. She was passionately keen for us to show her on our hired projector the little film that Aziz had shot of the two of us together in Venice, his fable of a melancholy young man (me) who meets his dark beloved (him) and the complex happiness that ensues. It must have been excruciating for her to watch, I now realise, although she insisted that she wanted nothing more in the whole world, and professed intense admiration for every frame. I had determined from the beginning to be honest about my emotional situation, honest with both of my triangular partners, but this seemed a little like rubbing all our noses in the dirt. Afterwards, Aziz wanted to take pictures of us all, but Peggy vehemently refused, and shortly after took a cab back to Earl's Court, taking with her the harlequin, at which she had barely glanced.

It was a turning point, a moment of truth for all of us. After it, I believe we all saw each other differently. We had to make a decision, either to carry on with all the complexities that had been thrown up, or to part company. It could have been the end of a number of things: my friendship with

Peggy, but also, to my amazement, it seemed to threaten the continuation of my relationship with Aziz. Next to Peggy, everyone seemed less: less passionate, less perceptive, less brilliant, less honest, less absolute. And Aziz had seen, not only how important Peggy was in my life, but a side of me, fervent and wild, which was only brought forth by Peggy. In fact my friendship with her survived that evening; grew stronger, if anything, as did my troubled love of Aziz and his anxious love of me. Some form of stock-taking was called for, however. I kicked off with a note to Peggy which intended to be bright but instead was full of palpable uneasiness. 'Dearest Dear Peggy, Isn't it odd us not writing to each other since that Friday? Was it such a potent encounter that we have to pause to take breath? One thing's for sure: nothing you said or did was not as it should have been. I don't think the evening was a failure at all: in one of the strangest situations never devised by a dramatist I think we all acquitted ourselves honourably, given that we none of us had any precedent to follow and were feeling our ways blindly. To start with, I'm simply delighted that you and Az have met each other, and I want you both to know each other properly and fully as each other and without reference to me. The tangled web of emotions that at present surrounds us, shooting off in all directions and in every conceivable permutation, is simply the occasion for us all having contacted each other. The rest is what will really count: what we do to and for each other as time goes on . . . and it will. We're not going to stand still, any of us.' Aziz wrote a charming formal note of thanks; and Peggy at first tried to be vivacious.

What a wonderful evening! I felt like the star in the show with my two beautiful escorts and the romantic restaurant and the revelation of the *need* you and Aziz have for one another, and seeing Aziz as he really is – deeply *deeply* worth while, and special. How extraordinary that you should have found each other at the time of your greatest need – the Harlequin is looking *wonderful* on my couch – I am dizzy at the thought that you should have bought it together and that you should have bought if *for me*. (You see what I mean about everything being the most wonderful 'bonus' if one supposes there is *nothing* – the 'nothing' is dynamic, *not* negative.) The Venice film! What a brilliant thing it was to turn your lives into ART.

Then she wrote a second letter, this time about Aziz, in short, breathless paragraphs:

Aziz is enchanting – like a jewel and so *young* and delicate to behold. Pitifully young. I understand your feelings!

IF he wants to meet me for a short time alone, it's because now I would like to know about his work and what he does in the cinema exactly.

Do you think I'd treat a delicate creature like that *wrongly?* You don't know me *at all.*

Dear Puppy

Yours Peggy

He's not at all what I expected.

PS My passion for you is like an airship – it is separate from me and I have to hold on to it or it would pull me up into the stratosphere.

I've bought a hat with a pheasant feather slashing across it – what shall I do with the hat? I should have passed a poulterers not a hat shop!

Now I've seen Aziz I am a little frightened for you . . .
I know so much more than you about you both. But I
LOVE your passion for him and I understand it perfectly
and I know exactly the bewilderment of your feelings.
I wave to you from my airship.
Oh how lucky I am that *you* should be my passion. I
regard this as supremely talented of me!!!!

Then she wrote a card to Aziz: 'Ziz – you were *so sweet* last
night. You are a *remarkable* person and I admire you so
much. Till we meet again,' and later wrote to him suggesting
that we use her garden to sleep in during the hot summer.
'As a child I slept out on the lawn once and I've never
forgotten it.' But deep inside her, something else was welling
up. 'I've felt bad about you both answering my questions
about your pasts so freely and then clamming up myself,'
she wrote. 'I remembered *one* incident in my Bertolucci-like
past, so here it is. While D.R.' – a contemporary of Peggy's,
a distinguished actress of whom we had spoken over supper
at Betty Martin's – 'was in a Rep, with decent people around
her who could see her through an abortion with the aid of
a friend's doctor and money, I was quite alone, with no
friends and living in a sordid room in S. Ken. When I
became pregnant the last thing I dreamed of doing was to tell
the man, or ask him for help. I found out the address of a
'doctor' in Tottenham Court Road – an awful old man in a
filthy room. There was an outer room with a lot of derelict
girls waiting and when I went in he told me he charged £1 a
session and I was to come every day. He added that *however*
ill I became I could not send for him, as he would not come.
He had a kind of dentist's chair and you were told to take off
your knickers and he injected you with a long syringe filled

– it seemed – with ether. You were then dismissed and you tottered down Tottenham Court Road till the next time. After a number of visits – as many as you could afford, and it often meant eating *or* going to him, you woke up one night – you were torn apart after a few hours (and you had to stifle the screams) the whole thing disembowelled. The place was like an abattoir and you had to find the bathroom and push this terrible thing into the lavatory. But when you returned, there was a *further* horror called it seems, the 'after' birth and which again had to be disposed of. You then had to wash away and dispose of any evidence and go on as if nothing had happened. Shortly after this the Doctor was arrested and a number of us were traced. As I had no passport (my husband had stolen mine) and I was a stranger in England, and under-age, I was taken into care instead of having to go to court and be convicted. I was sent to a house in Richmond – in a suburban street in a row of houses, where a religiously-led woman was in charge of a dozen or so girls in a similar predicament. No one knew who the other one was – first names only were told – for many weeks I had to live with these people. We were virtual prisoners in this house and were taken on walks in a kind of crocodile. Church services were held three times a day, by this woman and we were made to scrub floors, wash dishes, cook, sew etc. After a period – several weeks – you were released, provided someone vouched for you. As I had no one, I was allowed to go *only* provided I chose an 'approved' lodging. I was given – lent – a few pounds and agreed that when I got work I would pay it back – which I did later on. *Another* time I'll tell you about why I ran way from my husband and what became of him. I am telling you and Aziz what I have *never* told to anyone in the whole wide earth.'

41

I was so shaken by this letter that I was hardly capable of any meaningful reply. I was only slowly grasping the depth of Peggy's relationship to life, the grim underpinning of all her gaiety and audacity. From then on, the great themes of our friendship were established; love, art, jealousy, possession, repeated in over a thousand letters that we sent to each other, daily, sometimes twice and three times a day. I showed her letter to Aziz, of course, and he too was awed by it, more daunted than ever by Peggy. He went back to Geneva shortly afterwards, and we continued the international progress of our relationship.

5

There had been a tedious new development. When Aziz had tried to come back to England, he ran into a mysterious problem, never explained, with the Home Office, who refused to allow him to stay in the country for more than a week at a time. This offended and depressed him, and he vowed not to come back to Britain until they relented. Our relationship was then conducted across Europe and America in the gaps of my schedule at the National Theatre. We met in a succession of glamorous watering-holes, New York, Paris, Gstaad, Rome. It was in New York one frozen winter when we met there that I finally understood and accepted the reality, and the gravity, of his mental condition: New York, whose boundless energy I had hoped would prove contagious but which instead first threatened and then snuffed out his already fragile self-confidence. From the moment we met at the airport, it was clear that Aziz, unable to laugh, hardly able to talk, was in terrible trouble. He didn't want to go out; what he most wanted was to sleep. He had no appetite for food. If he drank, it was to achieve oblivion. This was depression in the clinical sense, and it was new and frightening. I felt quite powerless; there was nothing that I could do to reach the Aziz that I knew was there, somewhere, drowning in the inky fluid of despair.

Sometimes, for a few minutes, his former self would appear. I realised that life was taking a new turning, one that could never have been foreseen when we fell in love one sun-dappled summer, but I perfectly accepted it. It was like discovering that one's partner, or one's child, perhaps, had diabetes, or multiple sclerosis: there was no option, really, no question of ignoring it or running away from it. We'd just take it on board and forge ahead. If it didn't kill us, it would make us stronger. There was almost a sense of relief; at least the thing had a name. There would be avenues to explore, experts to consult. I felt, perhaps for the first time in my life, a sense of responsibility for another human being, and I eagerly embraced it. 'Another part of my destiny,' I wrote to Peggy from the friend's loft in which we were staying, 'is Aziz. He's not happy; in fact, I'd say, he's undergoing a protracted nervous breakdown. A lot of the time it's not much fun. Some of the time of course it's as wonderful as ever; but often his private numbness takes him over, poisoning his life and turning it into ashes. I'll tell you more later; but the point is, I embrace that too. This quiet agony (for both of us) must be gone through. DON'T worry about it, Peggy, or think that anything can be done now. It's slow and inexorable; but there is a light at the other end of the tunnel.' Somehow, the two weeks passed, with glum visits to the theatre and the galleries, and a little trip to Harvard to perform sonnets, where the snow drifts piling up vertiginously against the buildings seemed to Aziz's despairing mind even more terrifyingly to make external the frozen misery within him. We parted tenderly, but with fear on our souls, he returning to Geneva, to his grim little apartment, to his therapist, to his mother, I to London, the theatre, and Peggy.

She and I spent long, serious times together turning these events over and over; the pressure was reduced when he reported that the cycle had begun to swing upwards, and he was part of the human race again. Peggy and I also spoke frequently on the telephone, most often at night from the theatre during the runs of *Galileo* and *Sisterly Feelings*, when I was often in the dressing room for an hour at a time between my scenes. In the course of one of these conversations, I told her about my urgent need to move house. The friend who owned the flat in Notting Hill Gate in which I had been living decided that he needed to sell it and I was listlessly searching for an affordable place. Without pause Peggy said, 'Would you like me to give you a flat? I made a bit of a surplus this year.' I laughed. 'Why are you laughing?' 'It's a funny idea.' 'You mean, you wouldn't accept it?' I stopped laughing. 'Would you accept it?' 'Peggy, if you were to *lend* me . . . ' 'Don't be so bourgeois, dear.' The first unkind thing she had said to me, the first slap, of which there were to be many, many more over the years. 'You're not going to be boring about it, are you? I have the money, you need it, it's as simple as that. It means nothing to me. I've got nothing to spend the money on. You must be big enough to take it.' Then a change in her tone. 'Shall we go and look for flats tomorrow? Would that be nice? Would that be nice?' 'Very nice,' I said, and laughed again. 'Why are you laughing?' asked Peggy, but she was laughing too. 'You make it seem like fun,' I said. She beamed audibly. 'Yes,' she answered, 'that's what it is – fun.'

She immediately bombarded me with estate agents' circulars, while I trudged round their offices. Eventually, one blazing summer's day not much more than a week later, I was sitting in one, describing what I wanted, and how much I could afford: £25,000. That was what Peggy was giving me, an unimaginable amount for someone scraping

45

by on £180 a week at the National, though it was a modest sum, even then, in 1980, for a flat in town. They too seemed to have nothing. Then the assistant, peering unhopefully into the filing cabinet, saw something that had fallen down the back of the drawer, fished around for it and produced the details of 60, Finborough Road, a second-floor maisonette at the top of a large Victorian house in Earl's Court, on sale at precisely £25,000. It had fallen down eighteen months before, and was still on the market, at the same price. I called Peggy at the office; she immediately got into a cab and together we tottered up the three flights of stairs to inspect the airy, sun-drenched apartment in a mood of crazy exhilaration. She laughed a deep diaphragmatic chuckle when I walked into one of the modest little rooms and triumphantly declared, 'and this will be the Master Bedroom!' The flat backed onto Ifield Road, with its three excellent restaurants, which in turn backed onto the Brompton Cemetery. It was five minutes walk from Redcliffe Square, and sat on the big arterial road leading from the Embankment to the Westway, and literally quaked from the quantity of traffic which thundered down it day and night. That seemed all part of the excitement. We took the flat on the spot in the highest of spirits and I returned her to her office, my head reeling. A flat of my own! The exhilaration outweighed any sense of the oddity of the situation, of which the estate agents appeared to be quite oblivious. Perhaps they thought she was my mother.

It was a month or two before I took possession. During that time the exhilaration was slowly replaced by depression, a depression specifically related to the flat, one which lasted for a considerable period of time. To begin with, there was no chance, it seemed, of Aziz sharing it with me for the foreseeable future; his absence seemed emblematic of the capricious laws which kept us apart. In addition there were all my middle-class, my *bourgeois*, resistances to the idea of getting things which one had not earned – or, more specifically, to the idea of being *kept* (is there a word more offensive to the middle-class mind?). Finally, there was a feeling of having been overwhelmed in the relationship, of having lost the initiative, of having no equality within it. The flat symbolised something, and sometimes, for some little while after I had moved in, I would sit immobile, a stranger in it, oppressed by the very walls. I despised, too, my inability to rise to the grandeur of the gesture. I felt that I was small, petty, in the face of this generosity, not only financial, but personal, spiritual. I made a pusillanimous attempt at restoring my self-respect by trying to think of the £25,000 as a loan after all and establishing an account into which I should from time to time pay money. Peggy's scorn at this manoeuvre knew no limits. Finally, I overcame my resistance, gave up having qualms, and understood that the only way to deal with generosity is with generosity, resolving henceforth to pass through life myself with the same big spirit that had inspired her gift. Peggy's lessons to me were legion, but that was no doubt the greatest of them all. 'First,' I wrote to her, 'quite simply, the scale of your gesture is so gob-smacking that I've been a bit stunned by it, felt very passive in the fact of it. But that's all nonsense. This is the way I really see it: our lives are only controlled by us to the degree that we embrace our fate. We can resist destiny, make ourselves unavailable to its invitations and cut ourselves off from the pulse and onward movement of life (from the future and the ever onwards-and-upwards principle) or we can jump aboard; being the rider rather than the ridden, and always ready to change horses (or metaphors!) in mid-stream – but never to sit by the roadside or in the post-house. Well, I reckon that you're my destiny and I'm yours, in that sense. It's pointless to resist it, you didn't seek me; I didn't seek you. It was, as they say, in Robt. Bolt screenplays, WRITTEN. Allah. What fun; and thank god it was you, and thank god it was me. You've given me untold things, material and spiritual. I'm giving you whatever I've got, ditto. Sooner or later someone else will come along who'll need from me what I've been given by you; and I hope and pray that I'll do for him/her what you've done for me. In a way everything you've given me is in trust'.

The flat had been a kind of gauntlet flung down by Peggy: would I rise to the challenge? When I did, it became the physical manifestation of the bond between us. She had keys to it, ostensibly in case of emergency, but from the moment I moved into the flat, I could expect to find, every morning when I went downstairs to get the mail, a hand-delivered letter from Peggy, with an offering of foodstuffs, a cheese, perhaps, or a jar of soup made the night before, with a vase of flowers from her garden, snowdrops or anemones according to season. It was as if 60, Finborough Road were a shrine, and she was its votaress. One night while I was rehearsing Shaw's *Man of Destiny* for television I came home to find awaiting me on the staircase a large carrier bag containing a contemporary miniature of Napoleon painted while he was still on Corsica, two coins of his reign, a rare book about Venice, three Venetian concerti by Vivaldi, and a single of Peggy Lee singing the hit number from *How to Succeed in Business without Really Trying:* 'I believe in you.' The range of Peggy's passions was breathtaking, only matched by her generosity. I described all this to Aziz, longing to share it with him, anxious that he wouldn't feel overwhelmed by it all. It had nearly wiped me out; what might it do to him?

Peggy's obsession with me was not confined to property. In her enthusiasm to promote my development as an artist, Peggy had once offered me a sum of money, saying 'You mustn't have anything to worry you – not this year. This is an absolutely seminal year in your career, you do agree, don't you? And above all you mustn't do *anything* to make money, just to make money.' Courting accusations of being bourgeois, I refused, as, after the first couple of months of receiving red Mandarina Duck wallets stuffed with the currency of whichever country I might be going to, I refused all her gifts of money: I needed to make my own way. The flat was the only substantial gift I had from her that I did not – could not – match in some way. If she gave me a painting, I gave her a sculpture; when she gave me a tie, she got a handbag; my Schoenberg LP was provoked by her Zemlinsky cassette. Her overflowing generosity extended to work, too: she would often try to influence people to cast me in films and in plays, but as far as I know nothing came of these attempts. Once, very early in our relationship, she persuaded John Tydeman, head of drama on BBC Radio, to allow me to read a short story by the great newspaper Editor, Tom Hopkinson; they were broadcasting two, and Paul Scofield read the other one. My story, *Over the Bridge*, was a particular favourite of Peggy's, an extraordinary revelation of the madness caused by love, with its eerie ending: 'The paper I write on grows dim and hard to see. Only you are clear, lying in a bed I have not slept in, in the corner of a room I have never seen. Close as that room seems, I know that I have a great way to go before I can reach it, by a path that no one has walked before. As the candle goes out I shall leave my chair and walk across the room. The room is long but there is not more than ten yards for me to tread. The window is tall, taller than I am, and wide open. I have drawn the sofa up in front of it. I shall walk straight from my chair, step up upon the sofa, and move out from the window into the night sky.' It was as if I were reading it for her private hearing.

I was, as it seems to me now, to a remarkable degree unembarrassed by this patronage. I was dimly aware that it was the subject of comment, but the breadth of Peggy's spirit and the scale of her impulses seemed to protect me from any feeling of humiliation; I was sufficiently confident of my own worth to accept that Peggy was simply alerting people to my existence, rather than imposing me on them. Martin Sherman said at the time that we were a sort of literary *Harold and Maude* (he also once described me and Aziz as Amadeus and Cleopatra); but if that was the worst (in the back-biting worlds of theatre and film) anyone was going to say about this strange relationship then we were being let off the hook very lightly.

One day Peggy told me that Michael Codron, the outstanding theatre producer of the sixties, seventies and eighties, who always acknowledged the importance of Peggy's advice to him when he was starting out, and who applied to her for it to the very end of her life, wanted to meet me; where would I like to go? I suspected that I was being given the once-over by a concerned party. Hoping to keep things informal, I rather absurdly suggested that we eat at the Salt Beef Bar off Leicester Square, but instead we met at Goodwin's Court, where Peggy had arranged a sort of picnic for us. I was dimly aware that I was being scrutinised. Word was out that Peggy had a new fascination, and people who cared about her wanted to know if this was going to be a good thing or a bad. When I got to the office, Peggy was in a very excitable state, and I felt a little as if I were meeting her family for approval. She gave Codron and me too much to eat and far too much to drink, busily fluttering around us. I found him ironic and elegant but exceptionally cryptic. I blustered about a bit, trying to be funny and profound in equal doses, and falling flat on my face in both modes. Peggy beamed and chortled at my every fatuous utterance and Codron became ever more expressively silent. I remember the meal was rather shorter than lunch usually is, and I was extremely grateful for that. I felt that Codron, who had terminated it, had decided that I was a complete idiot, a gauche charlatan. Peggy seemed oblivious to the failure of the meal. I realised, to my astonishment, that far from being an opportunity for Codron to give me a once-over, the purpose of this office picnic had been for Peggy to show me off; she wanted people to know about our friendship. 'Both Howard and Hare, I think,' she wrote to me, 'suspect I have a slight feeling for *an actor* (I've scarcely mentioned your name). They are behaving *strangely* – Howard rang me up *every day* (for God's sake). Hare refers to you as 'the boy' in exactly the tone his Manager in Teeth'n'Smiles speaks to Maggie, his self-destructive heroine. After the preview of *Galileo* I asked 'What was he like?' (Gambon). Hare said 'The boy?' 'No, you ass, Gambon.' Bond is showering me with poems. I am to be firmly rescued from any possibility of taking any interest in the *other* side of the footlights.' Those closest to Peggy no doubt at first feared that I might try to exploit her. From quite an early point, however,

I think there was a general acceptance of the authenticity of what may have been thought of as an eccentric relationship but a harmless one; I was clearly not after her money or her influence. No one, as far as I was aware, knew about the flat in Finborough Road.

Aziz had now finally come back to England for a brief visit. Throughout all this time, Peggy was passionately involved with his situation, torn in many directions: filled with compassion for him, anxious about the effect his decline was having on me, while at the same time being nakedly jealous of the place he occupied in my heart and my life. On his occasional stays in Britain, I had started to give, for the first time in my life, little supper parties, to some extent for Aziz, to give him a chance to shine in an intimate context: he could meet people, show his films and get to know my friends better. In fact, this strategy of mine only caused him more distress. The flat itself, embodying Peggy's love for me, was profoundly daunting to him, and he failed to see it as the haven I had hoped it would be; in his fragile condition, its relative emptiness and undecorated quality oppressed him. It was exceptionally light and open, which is what had attracted me to it. His dark, cramped and very expensive apartment in Geneva was almost explicitly womb-like; the Finborough Road flat seemed to him to be a challenge, requiring decisions and commitment. The idea of having guests, too, far from relaxing him, filled him with terror. He generally pumped himself up for these events with a great deal of Carlsberg Special and in that state would throw himself into manic activity which amounted to a parody of host-ship, laying down joke place cards and dancing around everyone with hard-edged playfulness. On one unhappy occasion, I invited Peggy to eat with us; the other guests were a number of actors, most of whom Peggy knew. She was in an extraordinary mood and cut across every conversation, pursuing her own obsessive lines of inquiry. Finally, when, at my suggestion, Aziz was trying to show videos of his films, she sat in front of the television screen, blocking it out completely. She left as soon as she decently could. Next morning she wrote a card to me (on the tube) beginning 'dear Thesp,' in which first she denounced the actors present for their triviality, then added, surprisingly 'one reason I don't feel happy with actors is because there's a part of me wishes I'd not left the theatre – this is chiefly why I NEVER go back-stage and the intensely passionate discussion between you and Dan (Massey) had the same effect of regret on me.'

She continued, lethally: 'The business of 60 Fin is *hilarious*. While it's afforded you a convenient pad when yours was threatened, it has become the making of Aziz into a kind of Swiss Bourgeois Personality – pride in home, manic tidiness, obsession with "property" and loving "wife". For you it moved a puppy from his adorable kennel in Nott. Hill, into becoming a successful middle-class actor-dog, giving little dinner parties . . . you have an affinity with the life-style of RAYMOND Massey and his house-proud Adrianne!' I replied angrily, the first time I had ever answered her back: 'Really, if you think Aziz has settled into Swiss bourgeois respectability I must have expressed myself very badly. Nothing could be further from that than his present behaviour. He's mad, Peggy, not bourgeois. His interest in clearing up was only ever an outlet for the creativity of which he's been so afraid; now there's only a token genuflection to domesticity. He's hyperactively en-gaged – even as I write – on his play, of which he completed the first draft a couple of mornings ago at dawn, sitting on the patio; he's helping a colleague from the National Film School to write and translate a script from Breton's *Nadia*; scribbling, scribbling, scribbling; talking twenty to the dozen – ideas, theories, visions, dreams – sometimes seeing God, other times believing in nothing but Love – you get the picture. It's all rather exhausting and sometimes socially embarrassing (for both of us); but bourgeois it ain't – whatever that might be, anyway . . . I can't imagine what Raymond Massey's and Adrianne Allen's dinners were like, but I suppose they had something to do with a glamorous life, of which I know nothing and care less. On the wider issue of the domestic life, it seems to me that the only real courage required in life is putting things to the test, actually seeing something through – everybody knows what's wrong with this and that, every fool has his idea about the way things should really be done; but who has the courage to do it, to put his money where his mouth is? Well, I'm trying the hardest thing I've ever done in my life – to keep passion alive when the romantic circumstances which gave it birth have died; to find out what is really behind all that intoxication, if anything; and to make it take root instead of spiralling off in its exotic blooms, a cut flower which, once its petals have fallen off is thrown into the dustbin. Christ, it's hard work, but I don't really see what else one can do.'

All this was part of our curious triangular relationship. The moment Peggy had met Aziz, she had bought golden chains for each of us, with little gold discs inscribed with all three of our names in our own handwriting taken from letters we'd written. And we all three of us wore them. At around this time both Aziz's chain and mine had broken, and Peggy, on one of her dawn raids with flowers, food and the latest novel, had seen them lying on the table. In her present mood this seemed highly significant. 'Put all those little gold and silver broken chains through my letter box and I'll get them mended. You don't have to *wear* them, but I somehow feel ill at the idea that you have them lying there *broken* – there's something ugly about the idea, like your feeling of my writing you a letter in the *tube*. Of course you might have deliberately broken mine because you were hurt and angry at me, and are being generally "put off" me because, suddenly, people are turning against me as an agent (just as, for a long time, I was praised unjustifiably) and one has somehow to go on and endure all this and hope that somehow or other it can be lived through.' I sent her a present (I can't recall what) and she rallied. The sun came out again. 'What a wonderful prez – like old times? Yes, we must *endure* these terrible patches. OF COURSE I wasn't "off" you – I was just fighting to try and live *without* you! I'm not good at being one of a crowd, and sometimes I think you are a little like *My Last Duchess*!!! But it's because you are so FULL of love, and of life, and you MUST stretch yourself in every way and meet everyone you can, and love everyone. – I'm NO LONGER protecting myself, or jealous of the flat and you – and WHERE ARE THOSE CHAINS???'

And we were back on course. She bombarded me with flowers – 'It's not flowers I've ordered, it's *foliage*, as you'll see. *Jungle*. Oh *excess, excess*. I've damned nearly drowned the flat in trees. If they don't fit, *give them away* or call a cab and put at least one outside my door, and it can join mine. I must be MAD. I wanted you to have GREEN, but went too far' – and we listened to music again in Redcliffe Square, drinking exquisite wines from the cellar she made sure was always wonderfully well-stocked, listening as she said 'with all our antennae at the alert: *mescalin evenings.*' I sent her the latest *Tristan* as a preparation for our visit to the Coliseum to see it. 'Every morning at 7am Redcliffe Square gets an excerpt from *Tristan* – I play 2 sides and the house rocks – all doors and windows open.' She was now as full of joie de vivre as ever. Aziz meanwhile had had to go back to Switzerland again, courtesy of the Home Office, and our telephone conversations were increasingly doomy.

I spoke to Peggy about it whenever I could. She was gravely compassionate. One day she phoned me urgently at Broadcasting House, where I had been recording, summoning me to the office to speak to me on 'a matter of the utmost importance.' She had to see me, she said. 'I know *what is wrong* with Aziz. I know; and I'm right. I may not charge £25 an hour, but I know about this.' When I got to the office, she started straight in, without preamble. 'About Aziz. It's you, you see. You've done it to him. You demanded total commitment – that was all he had to give. He's given everything now and there's nothing for him to do but lapse into a sort of trance. You exercised your overwhelming will on him, and he submitted. You fell in love with him with utter passion and when he wouldn't return it we both said, "How honest, how truthful of him." But he knew that he mustn't, that he couldn't. Now he's become – I'm going to be brutal now, can you take it? – he's become nothing but your catamite. You see you're so powerful, your will is so ENORMOUS. He's not like that at all. You've been trying to build him up to your level. You wanted him to make a career like yours – but that's impossible for him. He has a beautiful, an exquisite little talent – not like yours at all. He's like a flower. I saw it the other night when I said to him "Simon gives, gives, gives. He must

56

learn to take," and he replied "Oh he *does* take." I saw it immediately. He meant he's taken *me*. And you have. He *whispered* it. I'm not mistaken, you were there. This is not to say you can't have a relationship with him, you can, but not this one.' Then she described a favourite Thomas Mann short story of hers to me, concerning a man and his dog. 'He saw the dog, he fell in love with it, he got it, he covered it with love; and eventually the dog jumped out of the window. You don't know, you see, how POWERFUL you are, how STRONG. I'm strong too, in a way, so I can stand up to you – but he can't. You must let him have his freedom.' Reeling from the implications of all this, I numbly told her that however it had come about, the relationship was now essential to him, and that to lose it would possibly push him to desperate measures, a repeat, perhaps, of the several unsuccessful attempts at suicide that had figured in his past. 'Of course he won't commit suicide,' she said blithely, 'not if he KNOWS what's happened to him.' I had a terrible feeling that she might be right about me, about what I had done to Aziz in the name of love. I had no idea what to do about it, but simply carried on the only way I knew how, by working.

6

It was while I was nearing the end of my time at the National Theatre that Peggy made another of her uniquely magnificent gestures, capping, if that were possible, the gift of the flat. She gave me, in effect, a production: *Total Eclipse*, by her client Christopher Hampton. Long before I became an actor, I had seen the original production at the Royal Court, with Victor Henry, whom I knew slightly at the time, as a shattering Rimbaud. The play, about the love affair between Rimbaud and Verlaine, had stunned me with its frank depiction of that famous, sexually-driven relationship; plays about such subjects were uncommon in 1968. But it was to the part of Verlaine, sensuous, sentimental, selfish, that I responded most deeply, recognising in myself both his physical self-indulgence and his unswerving romanticism. From that time on, it had been the part I had wanted to play above all others, and I had told Peggy so in one of our earliest conversations. I was therefore electrified when she phoned me one afternoon in 1980 to say that she had been sitting with Christopher Hampton in his garden in Oxford that weekend and he had told her that he had always wanted me to play the part, that David Hare longed to direct me in it and that Michael Codron couldn't wait to produce it for me. I was amazed and delighted that they should have such warm feelings towards me, and decided to leave the National Theatre on the strength of it. Seemingly effortlessly, the play went on at the Lyric Theatre in Hammersmith, and it was an extraordinary experience, tragic, tender and funny, in a production exquisitely directed by Hare, luminously designed by Hayden Griffin, with torrid César Franck-like string music written by Nick Bîcat: a production of all the talents.

Rehearsals were happy, and I reported to Peggy on the show's progress in daily letters. In the rehearsal room, in a box of bric-à-brac destined for the jumble sale, I found a book of essays by Charles Morgan in which he quoted one of Verlaine's few poems in English, which filled us both with delight:

> I'm bor'd immensely
> In this buffet of Calais,
> Supposing to be, me, your lover
> Loved, – if true? – you are please
> To weep in my absence
> Aggravated by a telegram
> Tiresome where I count and count
> My own bores for your sake
> But what is morrow to me?
> I start to morrow to London
> For your sake, it, then, suddenly
> That sadness, so heavy, falls down

My birthday occurred somewhere in the midst of rehearsals, and Peggy had got me a present of more than usual munificence, full of resonance for both of us: a pencil sketch of Diaghilev as a Centaur, nine inches by ten and a half, made in 1910, by Chaliapine in a Paris café. The provenance said: 'In 1909 Serov drew Chaliapine as a Centaur with two wives. The singer borrowed the same theme for this caricature of Diaghilev, naturally omitting the wives.' Peggy described it: 'Hooves raised, a monocle and a tail like a plume; his two little balls like cherries and his little prick lying quietly between them – very demurely...it's in an *unsuitable* frame, particularly the mount, and you and Ziz must re-frame it to your liking. It's *not* 'decorative' but when one realizes that Chaliapine must have sketched it rapidly *on this very paper,* probably while they were sharing a meal, and that Diaghilev held it in his hand and must have laughed with pleasure. I don't know how it was preserved to reach us but it's for your birthday, and yours.' And then she added: 'Chaliapine says: "Love is always happiness, no matter what we love, but love for art is the greatest of all".' That summer love was everywhere: in her, in me, in Aziz (who was around through all the rehearsal period) and in the play. It was all bound up together. Aziz was happy to know that I had him fixed in my mind when I spoke Verlaine's exquisite final evocation of Rimbaud, his 'radiant sin', at the end of the play: 'When we walked in, he was standing with his back to us. He turned round and spoke, and then I saw him, and was amazed at how beautiful he looked. ' Nothing made him happier than when he knew that he somehow figured in my work. In *Total Eclipse* I had drawn on innumerable details in our relationship, but in fact everything that I was able to do in the role was part of that great thawing of emotion in me that he had caused. And Peggy was in there, too, not simply as organiser of the whole event, but as the keeper of the flame: she thoroughly approved of the relationship between Verlaine and Rimbaud, cauterising and transcendent. In one of her notes, Peggy sent me a letter she had written nearly fifteen years earlier to the twenty-one-year-old Hampton when he wrestling with the material: 'We aren't just talking about a homosexual relationship between two men who happen to be poets. We are talking about immortal poetry. I know great artists are petty, but this isn't a basis for a deeply moving play; it's Somerset Maugham country...Verlaine, from the start, worshipped Rimbaud's talent, and even in the end, a sodden mess, he must still hold something divine within him.'

She was deeply involved in this production of *Total Eclipse* at every level. There was a crisis over the music; the budget was not adequate, so Peggy simply wrote a cheque for £1,000 for it. In addition, she had decided to throw a party for the First Night, and most of her return letters to me concerned the composition of the guest list. This became her obsession. Virtually every writer, director and producer of note (no actors) was considered at one time or another. The list was finally reduced to manageable numbers; even so, that night after the show the basement flat in Redcliffe Square was positively bursting with talent and fame – Alan Bennett, Stephen Frears, Ronald Eyre at a glance: it was a sort of theatrical Debrett's. The Button padded in, and then swiftly padded out again, appalled. I passed among the guests in a daze, never having been in the same room at the same time with quite so many formidable talents. They in turn looked at me with wry curiosity, as Peggy, super-charged, played the hostess – none too comfortably, it seemed to me. I had never seen her throw a party before, and certainly she never threw one again; it was not really her style. She hated attending them. She had thrown this one simply because she believed, quite mistakenly, as it happens, that it was what I craved. She herself had not come to the show, staying at home partly to catch my performance as Napoleon in *The Man of Destiny*, transmitted on television that night, but mostly to transform the flat into a glittering salon: lamps large and small had been hauled in from every room transforming the room's habitual beige and oatmeal twilight into a hall of lights and mirrors; it became Versailles for the night. At the party Aziz behaved like an exquisite courtier, though nearly crippled with shyness; he and a somewhat drained Christopher Hampton found themselves sitting side by side on the sofa, and discovered that they had as children gone to the same school in Alexandria, a suitably exotic discovery for a very exotic evening, which went on and on, till Aziz and I and Peggy were left alone, clearing up, a little bashful with each other now in the sudden emptiness and silence of the flat. After tender and shy farewells to Peggy and expressions of gratitude – 'Was it fun? Was it fun?' she demanded over and over – Aziz and I trailed off to Finborough Road, able to talk about the show at last. It had moved him to the core. I went to bed deeply happy, *Total Eclipse* achieved, Peggy five minutes away and Aziz wrapped up in my arms. It was Guitry's prescription from *Deburau* (which Aziz and I had seen together in Paris) in which the ageing mime instructs his son just before he goes on stage: 'Love without work – not bad; but it's not a lot. Work without love? Hardly better. If you want a taste of paradise – I know what I'm talking about – try for both. When the show's over – go home and make love!'

The next morning brought an abrupt end to the idyll. The reviews were scarcely better than they had been on its first outing. Michael Coveney wrote a fairly enthusiastic piece for the *Financial Times*, which Peggy gallantly had blown up and framed and put on her office wall; she gave me a framed copy, too, but I never had the heart to put it up. Business was poor, but I never ceased to love being Verlaine. I wrote to Peggy after the first night thanking her for the party and for everything else connected with the show. 'What I want you to know is that my Verlaine bears a twin dedication: to Paul-Marie Verlaine and Margaret Ramsay, with love and passionate understanding. Without being too grand about it, I tried so hard to make the performance as direct a celebration of passion as I could – and a crystallisation of everything you and I have shared together – art, love, exaltation. So it's yours, Peggy, my Paul-Marie Verlaine. Every time he sets foot on the trembling revolve of the Lyric Hammersmith, a candle is lit for you.' She visited the show often (it was 'our show'), reading into it an allegory of what I meant to her. 'Strange that you are Verlaine each evening – the man who dedicated his later life to *the past* and who loved a man who lived *for the future*. You are a mixture of both these men…which enables you to pursue your work like an arrow from a bow, pulling out all the reserves of passion within you, the passionate quest for the future.'

She watched the performance grow over the run, mostly with approval. She was, however, highly displeased when she re-visited the play towards the end of the run and found, or thought she found, that I was playing Verlaine as if he loved his wife more than he loved Rimbaud. I was certainly greatly enjoying the scenes with Mathilde because of the rapport I had with Lindsay Baxter, who was playing the part, and I suspect that Peggy was jealous of her, jealous of her as an actress, jealous of the rapport between us, jealous of the physical contact; jealous even, in some way, of

Mathilde Verlaine herself. 'I have been burying my feelings for some months,' she wrote, 'in order to be able to function at all in my way of life where there is no emotional relief. My feelings have not altered at all – I think about you so much of the day and night, that you fill my secret life. But I have to keep it secret – from you too. Perhaps I shall allow myself to thaw a little when the sun begins to shine. Already in my garden the trees and flowers are alive again and are bursting into life. But at the moment my poet is Baudelaire: la tonnerre et la pluie.'

Somehow we were forging a modus vivendi, keeping faith with each other despite the impossibility of the situation. There had been one alarming incident between us, however, during the rehearsal period of the play. One evening after rehearsals, when Peggy and I were having a drink at Redcliffe Square, I innocently referred to the genesis of the production, wishing that shows could more often come into existence in that day-follows-night kind of way: writer wants actor, actor loves play, actor admires director and so on. Peggy exploded with sudden and alarming savagery, so much so that I beat a swift retreat. A letter was waiting for me on the doormat the next morning when I went to collect the milk.

'I'm unutterably depressed by your "memory" of how *Total Eclipse* came into being,' she raged. 'Chris has never ever thought of or mentioned any possible revival of the play in England. Nor at that time was he thinking of you as Verlaine. Why should he be? We spent an evening together and you told me the various things you wanted to do – you mentioned your Verlaine wish because we were looking through bookshelves. I, next day, phoned Chris and he was incredulous, as he saw the play had failed here and no one would do it. At that time you weren't a "name" either. Chris liked the idea of your doing it very much. I then saw Hare and he hesitated but then agreed. Hare said OK if Chris would re-write. Whose idea was it, then, about the revival? Hare? Are you suggesting Chris did it? The whole thing is cock-eyed in your memory. I set it up because you said you'd like to do it. Chris was asked for permission, nothing more. Anyway, I'm too fed up to continue this topic. Thinking about a play, choosing directors and actors is an *agent's job*. Oh let's drop the subject. If it pleases you to think that Chris thought of you for Verlaine, that he then talked to me, then he got Hare, and he got the Lyric Hammersmith - so fucking be it. It's because you fancy Chris that you want it this way. The idea that Chris rang me up to say "I've been thinking of *Total Eclipse*," or "I've been thinking of Simon Callow as Verlaine" is an absolute joke. WHO was he thinking would do the play? Where? How? It was a kind of miracle that the Lyric Hammersmith, under a new régime at that exact time, was sympathetic. After we'd got the Lyric to say yes (I say "we" as you may think Chris got it) Hare did *everything* else: got the play revised, the designs, the music - *everything*. But you accepted the part because you fancy Hare even more. I had nothing *whatever* to do with the play once it was given to Hare and the theatre booked it - until I had to pay for the music or do you think Chris paid for it? Don't answer this letter. Let's let time pass for a bit.'

More confused than hurt - perhaps I had indeed mis-remembered - I immediately went to see her the following evening and the storm passed: 'Sweetest Chuck,' she wrote, 'how sweet of you to come round last night. My *amour propre* wasn't dented. I was mourning your memory, which is far more important to me. But coming round and spending some time *à deux* was an especially adorable thing to do.' She ended the letter, somewhat redundantly, perhaps: 'how vulnerable we all are – Hare, you, I.' Years later, when I came to write this book, I looked back through all our correspondence for the first time, and came upon a letter of hers shortly after our first meeting, in which she says: 'I want to talk about your doing *Total Eclipse* somewhere, sometime. Hampton has always wanted you for Verlaine and Hare wants to direct it for you, and it could be done either at the NT or somewhere like the Riverside Hammersmith (Peter Gill my client) – it's really up to you.' Of course it was no such thing; she had told them that this was what they should be doing, and they did it. She then presented it to me in a way that wouldn't make me feel that it was an arranged thing, and I believed her; believed that these distinguished gentlemen were secret admirers of mine. Her sudden outburst at my naïvety was a primitive protest against being taken for granted, taken for a ride. Her charming fiction about the origins of the production was only useful as long as it was, however tacitly, understood to be a fiction. I did not make the same mistake again.

7

Total Eclipse ended its brief run at the Lyric Hammersmith. The decision not to transfer it was unavoidable, and Michael Codron broke it to me gently and sadly over lunch at the Garrick Club. The project was conceived in love and executed with love; those who saw it – including on one unforgettable occasion the tiny, shrunken but still dapper figure of the greatest actor of the twentieth century, Laurence Olivier, accompanied by his nurse, his massively magnifying spectacles twinkling in the stalls – on the whole loved it. But love was not enough, and the show expired quietly after four weeks. Peggy was a little shaken by its failure to catch on; she had believed that the play's time had come, and she believed passionately that my performance would be acclaimed to the very heavens. Neither proved true. Meanwhile, I had been asked by Edward Bond, another of Peggy's clients, to appear in his new play *Restoration*, which he was directing himself at the Royal Court. I have no idea whether she influenced him in casting me; there were strenuous sessions with him before I was given the part, so there was at any rate no question of him taking me on spec, or merely as a result of her opinion. He was, and is, a formidably uncompromising figure, and I imagined that everything that I was, and am, would be anathema to him, but in fact we had an unexpectedly exhilarating time together. Our point of contact, of course, was the theatre, his feelings for which proved to be almost as romantic as mine. The point at which we lost touch was his sense of what the theatre was for.

My quest to use the stage to celebrate the richness, diversity and sheer oddity of the human race was at odds with his determination to focus all its efforts on changing it. Increasingly, it seemed to me, he saw the stage as a platform or a pulpit, plays as pamphlets. At least, one part of him did; the other part, the dramatist of genius, was in the grip of a creative fever which led him to bold experiments with language – each of his plays up to and including *Restoration* had been written in a newly-forged style appropriate to each individual play – and to the creation of characters of an originality and a depth that had scarcely been seen on the English stage since the classical period. When he wrote these characters, he told me, they took him over; he never knew where they would lead him. This is of course is what gave them their staggering vitality. They were bigger than their author. When I asked him where the name of the character I was to play in *Restoration*, Lord Are, had come from, he said 'that's all he would tell me' – R, the initial of his family name. This was scarcely the method of the severe rationalist he purported to be. The division between Edward the dramatist and Edward the teacher (with added contributions from Edward the theorist) was absolute, and led to grief in the rehearsal room. Directing by means of homily and parable, he seemed to refuse to understand the problems that we had as actors – refused, I think on theoretical or even political grounds, to acknowledge that there was anything special about the task we were engaged on. I personally found the part of Are, which I knew to be one of the supreme roles of the modern theatre, almost impossible to play to my satisfaction or the author's, and, as is my wont, I flailed around, desperately attempting anything at all that would give me taste of the man I was trying to bring to life. 'No, no, no,' was all he would offer by way of encouragement. It was hell. I felt like a fool and a fraud.

Peggy and I endlessly discussed what was going on. She found him exasperating beyond belief, while admiring his integrity; she also had a soft spot for him personally. 'Little Bond,' she would call him, tenderly, 'why does he behave so disgracefully?' I wrote to her from the depths of despair: 'I've learned to take it as a very ominous sign when he says nothing and seems to approve. It's just when one's sailing gaily along apparently basking in the sunshine that the great axe falls. "I don't know what you're doing," he says tetchily. "It's so leaden." "What do you think about what you're saying? I can't understand," and so on. He worries away at one till one begins to wonder why one was born, let alone why one took up acting, not even to mention why one chose to do this wretched play. This wretched play, by the way, is without question the best non-classical play I've worked on. I don't know why I call it non-classical. It is classical. It's a new classic. That's all. Time is short. I think I'm going to get there, remorselessly prodded by Edward; but it's a huge play, containing a whole world, in its way the whole world. God, how Edw. would hate to hear me talk like that.'

Things began to get very tense in the rehearsal room and around the theatre when we moved there. The set seemed not to be working as planned; the integration of the songs with the play was not without its difficulties, either, and Bond was not skilled at providing solutions to these problems. He had long ago taken a decision to direct his own new plays, but he had not, I felt, taken the next decision, to learn the craft of directing, any more than he was in the least interested in understanding the craft of acting. It seemed to him that if he expressed the point of the play clearly enough, everything would fall into place. Predictably, it didn't. The previews, though clumsy, went well enough; somehow we arrived at the first night, though Bond himself was not present to see it, which did nothing to endear him further to an already disaffected company. Aziz was at the opening, allowed himself to get rather more drunk than he should have and failed to follow the elaborate language and extravagant situations; he returned the following night stone-cold sober, and was not much the wiser. It was not the sort of play that he was ever likely to enjoy, and my performance, on a very grand scale, left him, I think, rather cold. This was perfectly all right by me, though it disappointed him. I respected his failure to be ignited by it, because in my heart, despite excellent reviews and lively audiences, I knew that even though I had finally mastered the part, the effort showed, and effort was the one thing that the character should have been free of. And then Aziz was back off to Geneva again, like a fugitive from justice, and I settled in to the rigours of the run, trying to refine what I had arrived at by the first night, but in fact only coarsening it.

I talked to Peggy endlessly about the frustrations of the experience; eventually, after a performance which was very sparsely attended on account of the Royal Wedding (Charles and Diana), all the holes in the production opened up, no longer covered by the roar of a large audience. Furious and drunk, I sat down and wrote Edward a letter berating him for not allowing his play be as good as it should have been. In the morning, I re-wrote the letter more coherently, on the green paper which I affected at the time, but I was suddenly nervous of delivering it to Bond: who was I to tell this great writer, and so on. So I showed it to Peggy. 'It's a very *important* letter,' she said. 'You must send it.' I demurred, at which she pulled a stamp out of the drawer of her desk saying, 'Don't be a coward. Send the letter. You must help to save Bond from himself.' I promised I would give it to him when I saw him next. In case I thought I was off the hook, she followed this up with a hortatory letter: 'Bond is obviously upset because he must know the play doesn't work altogether, but he justifies it by saying that *no one* else can do it, and that only time was needed to get his production perfect. So you MUST try to send that letter – or he will *destroy his career* by doing this kind of thing again.' She had told him, she added, that I'd written him a letter and that he must insist on reading it. 'You will have seen him Saturday night I'm sure as I talked to him and that everything is now OK between you.'

He duly came to the Saturday performance which went better than it ever had. The letter suddenly seemed redundant. Bond came up to me, his eyes twinkling, and said that apparently I'd written him 'a green letter'. I was disinclined to spoil the warm glow created by the show that night and said, 'It's a horrible letter,' to which he replied, 'Then you'd definitely better give it to me.' I said, 'I do happen to have it with me.' He blanched and said, 'Would you do me a favour, would you send it to me?' and I, relieved that I didn't have to hand it to him there and then, said yes, I would. We then walked round Sloane Square, talking of this and that, and then quite unexpectedly he invited me to eat with him. We went to Como Lario, and had a delightful, passionate and rather funny conversation, in the course of which I imparted some unpalatable truths which he took graciously, offering me a few in return. 'We found,' I wrote to Peggy, 'that we had one very important thing in common: a conviction that though we were both rather better at our respective jobs than some of the people around us, we both felt that we were only at the beginning. He said to me, "I am determined to be a good writer. I will be by the time I die. At least I shall be able to say that." And then he asked for the poisoned letter. I gave it to him with many qualifications, which he poohpoohed, saying, "I can always throw it out of the window." Next morning, he phoned very early and left a message on my machine saying that he'd read it, that it was a kind and generous letter, that he was glad I'd written it and glad that he'd read it, and of course he agreed with it absolutely, and that he'd reply to it point by point.' Of course he never did.

Peggy was pleased that he'd read the letter, but he was still in the doghouse as far as she was concerned. 'I am speechless with rage over Edward,' she wrote, a week later. 'I didn't dare to tell you about it.' Bond had wanted a recording of the songs from the show and suggested a three-hour band call on the final Saturday morning before the matinée. 'I said "Who is going to pay?" He said "I hear you've given the Court some money for a small party – I'd prefer that money to be used for taping the show." I blew my top and said he was the most selfish thoughtless person I'd ever encountered and his contempt and indifference to actors *appalled* me. WHY should they give up their Saturday and not get paid, and to try and take their little party money seemed *appalling*.' There was no recording, and we did have a party, which he didn't attend. Edward's behaviour was perfectly consistent, motivated by one thing and one alone: his belief that the work, the play itself, that is, and the production, was more important than anything or anyone else, including himself. It was self-evident to him that if there were to be a choice between a party and a recording of the work, everyone would agree that the work must prevail. He had none of the feeling for the company and the traditional observances that Peggy had; all that seemed to him irrelevant and culpably bourgeois.

The violence of her feeling about Bond's bad behaviour was a part of a general sense of doom which we shared around this time. 'The last couple of months,' I wrote, 'have been killers, from every point of view; work, life, the world. I've felt lousy at my job, incapable of sustaining friendships, rejected by people I love, and feeling that they were right, I deserved rejection. I particularly felt that YOU had seen through me, were fed up and bored by the idea of me, thought your whole involvement with me had been a mistake. Because I didn't hear from you after you came to the last preview of *Restoration*, I assumed that you thought that even my acting had gone to pot. And certainly, during the worst times during the rehearsal period, I really desperately cast around for an alternative profession, as I was obviously so inadequate at this one. There have been days and days of grey emptiness, nothing to do with being busy; simply hurtling around with nothing inside me but a kind of fog.' If I was down, she was in a mood of apocalyptic depression. She was experiencing acute misery over a play of Jack Rosenthal's (*Smash*) which had closed out of town and whose failure and the attendant recriminations and reproaches had made her doubt herself in a way I had never seen before; she who had said with such utter certainty when I first met her that if ever she had made an error of judgement in her work, she would have retired immediately.

'I feel to be an agent is something *disgusting* at the moment and I don't know what I should do. I'm not really fit to mix with people! I'm not quite sure *why* the times seem so bad for us all. You feel your beloved theatre is being relegated to an unimportant pastime and this is just part of a general indifference to everything – and you are right, and it's our fault, and part of the symptoms of the sickness. The trouble is that all of us (not you) are turning away from loving understanding. How all these things are poisoning and destroying us. Turning to small acts of cruelty to *attack* is a kind of self-defence . . . this is all part of the same sickness, which is affecting so many of us, and which turns into an ugly kind of destructiveness.' She thought she knew why. 'I've been trying to "cure" myself of my affection for you, and in some way putting barriers up, so that it will be impossible for us to meet – hence the letter after that nice dinner party, followed by the letter attacking your other dinner parties, but the flat too, so that there will be nowhere where we can meet. During these last weeks, for the *first* time,' she continued, frighteningly, 'I considered killing myself – not just on impulse, but a continued contemplation of some way to do it. I even met Harbottle to re-write my Will (something I had to force myself to do) and included a plan about how to hand over the office and have my name removed forever as soon as possible after I died. I'm waiting for the final documents now.'

Somehow – for no real reason, simply because our mood changed – we both cheered up shortly afterwards. On the professional front there was improvement for her: 'Jack phoned today to say that I was more important than the play, and I said we'd both try and start again from the beginning and gel the play BETTER – there is so *much* lacking in it: like *Loot* first time round.' I meanwhile was getting under the skin of Beefy in *The Beastly Beatitudes of Balthasar B*, the most joyful of all the many life-drunk creations of that Irish-American lord of misrule, J.P. Donleavy. Simply working on the character cheered me up no end. Donleavy had made a play from his novel about the melancholy journey through life of the exquisite Balthasar and the occasional riotous irruptions into it of his schoolboy chum, Beefy – Beefy the lyrical and profane, priapist and poet, spreader of equal quantities of joy and mayhem. Through the course of the action he slowly descends into humiliation and economic ruin, though his soul, and other working parts, remain intact. Four years before, John Dexter had asked me to play the part for him, but the project had foundered; the introduction to Dexter, however, led to him asking me to play Mozart in *Amadeus*, so I had reason to be grateful to Beefy even before Patrick Ryecart approached me to play him in the West End. Pat, passionate to play Balthasar, had, with remarkable entrepreneurial audacity, persuaded the elusive Donleavy to give him the rights, though he had never put a play on before. Together we set up a production, and even before *Restoration* had ended its run, we were in rehearsal with *Balthasar*.

Nothing could have been further from Edward Bond's world, or his world view. Romantic, nostalgic, snobbish, mellow, written in great soaring melodious paragraphs whose meaning was sometimes secondary to their music, it was a perfect Cavalier dipole to Bond's Roundhead linearities. Beefy was for me the crowning glory of the three extraordinary parts I had played since leaving the National Theatre. If Verlaine in all his complex and contradictory impulses was rather dangerously close to the real me, and Lord Are, certain, ruthless, and demonic, utterly alien from my normal self, Beefy really was the me of my dreams, crying yes to life, and damn the consequences. Nothing human is strange to him; he is a blessing in flesh. I never really seemed to need to play Beefy; he seemed to be playing me. Donleavy's great coloratura speeches poured out effortlessly: this was the celebration of innocence, prelapsarian grace and sweetness and fun, and I often found myself weeping, as I sat at home working on the script, at the sheer sunny kindness and goodness that Donleavy was dispensing through Beefy. I never in my life more wanted an audience to meet the character I was playing, wanted them to get to know him. It was a golden summer as we rehearsed in our church hall in Maida Vale, and I got happier with every passing day.

Eventually the posters and billboards went up outside the Duke of York's Theatre in St Martin's Lane, only two minutes away from Peggy's office in Goodwin's Court. She had thus seen the posters before I did, and had immediately flown into a rage. The management had determined, no doubt rightly, that neither Pat nor I were the selling points of the show at that point in our careers, so prominence was given to Donleavy's name and that of the play; and this threw Peggy into a rage. Unluckily for him, the producer, Bill Freedman, had an office next to hers in Goodwin Court. 'I must warn you I've had a hell of a confrontation with Bill your manager,' she wrote. 'I said I thought it *disgraceful* you and your partner didn't get publicity, that your billing was too small, that your salaries a disgrace. I said *you* got the Duke of York's, and you and P got the play and that if they wanted to be good managers, they should treat actors with *respect*. I also said you were a *draw* and if the play succeeded it would be YOU and P,' which was touching, but sadly untrue, as *Total Eclipse*, in my case, had definitively proved. 'He was overwhelmed with my attack,' she added, perhaps unnecessarily, 'and I told him you knew nothing of it but that the whole of the theatre WOULD unless he treated you properly!'

For the first time, I wondered whether Peggy's passionate promotion of my talents might be a mixed blessing. Fortunately, everyone behaved calmly; the posters were eventually changed, and in due course we appeared in front of an audience for the first time, I with my hair dyed the carrotty red so vividly described by the author. In the stalls at that first preview, unknown to me, was Peggy. '11.30pm Wednesday. I saw the play tonight and it is one of the most touching and lyrical things I've seen – beautiful – transformed by love and care. Patrick could be a little more confident and he'll be lovely. I *loved* you: far better than the Bond play which seemed somehow strained. The trouble is that if you get the notices you deserve it will run for the nine months – I really hate to feel vengeful about a management who could treat you as they have done – they will regret it, and will soon give you the billing you deserve.'

Aziz was also at that first preview. He was living on borrowed time in London; the Home Office had rejected the appeal that our solicitor, Laurence Harbottle, had made on his behalf, and had decreed, with impeccable timing, that he was to return to Geneva on 23rd October, the day of the first preview. Harbottle advised against a further appeal because there seemed to be some kind of blacklist, and Aziz, mysteriously, appeared to be on it. Harbottle's further advice was to lodge a new appeal from Switzerland; the authorities (whoever they might be: this was Kafka-land) felt that there was a pistol at their temples if an application came from someone who'd already been granted a visa. Somehow they were persuaded to extend his permit by a week, so he was there, triumphantly if somewhat angrily. His delight in the show and particularly my work was complete; this is the way he liked me to be: affirming, embracing, fleshly (although he admitted that he found the scene when I appeared naked apart from a driving hat, goggles and a number of chains 'a little rude'). Audiences during the preview period rather liked this moment; in fact, they were riotously appreciative throughout. On one occasion a couple in the stage box were so infected by the spirit of the play that they slid slowly to the floor and started putting into practice what Beefy was so energetically preaching. Peggy came again to the last preview, and uttered a warning: 'It's all grown immensely,' she wrote, 'but you are on a knife-edge of coarsening the part – take care.' With the letter was an extraordinary bottle of Grappa, with what looked like a small tree growing inside it. I wrote back to her the next day, just hours before the performance on the First Night, agreeing that there was 'the most awful potential for Donald McGillery'. I was fighting it, I said, with every fibre of my being, but had been in trouble vocally, battling with a super-production of mucous, which was taking away the whole of my upper register, and limiting my voice to one note. I knew that she was right, however. 'Voice or no voice, the tendency to end up on the end of the pier will be resisted at all costs.'

Perhaps I wasn't able to resist that tendency; for whatever reason, the First Night was a cheerless occasion. 'One of the most dreadful houses on an opening I've ever known,' I wrote to Peggy, adding, clearly over-exposed to Donleavy, 'fuckpigs of multiplicities'. It was a curious event, Aziz determined to have a good time and to buoy me up before his enforced exile, and accordingly and dangerously awash with Carlsberg Special. Between that and the adrenaline of a first night, against a background of a deepening and darkening sense of his inability to grasp his own life, he was on a tight-rope, delicately swaying above a dreadful chasm. It was terrible to watch, and impossible to help. He returned to Switzerland soon after the opening, unsure of when if ever if he would be allowed to come back. This was distressing for me – would I be able to get away at all to see him, with eight performances a week? – but worse than distressing for him: it was profoundly disturbing, adding to his sense of rejection and alienation (where did he belong?), now on an international level.

I meanwhile was wallowing in rage and disappointment at the rather poor press that *Balthasar* had received. 'Well, they seem to be getting better,' I wrote to Peggy. 'Coveney's savagery was a little bit unexpected, de Jongh's mean-spiritedness predictable but nonetheless upsetting – is there a more deeply foul thing you can say about an actor's performance than that it is selfish? I was very upset. Pat, I'm privately informed, cried when he read the FT. By lunchtime his indestructible spirit had revived, and by night he was positively cocky. "What it all boils down to," he said, "is that they wish they'd been born with blond hair and blue eyes".' Unlike him, I went on brooding, as actors have done from time immemorial, at the injustice of it all. 'We might have succeeded or failed, but what lies behind the raging contempt? I don't think its very worst enemy would claim that the play, show I suppose is a more accurate word, is in any way cynical or ungenerous. It's flawed, no doubt, all the way round, me, Pat, the set, the direction, smaller parts and so on, but through it there does flow a spirit of good-heartedness, of openness and celebration.'

Peggy had no time at all for any of this. 'I can't refer in detail to your railings against the critics. All I can do is to beg you to get a sense of *proportion*. Beefy is not Iago, and the play isn't comparable to *Othello*. NO ACTOR CAN really be better than his play, and you have performed a miracle in making this material into a really funny, touching little play . . . the trouble is that you fell in love with Beefy, who is adorable and funny as you play him, but this isn't *enough* for a chorus of praise from the West End critics – you want them ALL to scream MARVELLOUS – but the play is very slight and *isn't* a masterpiece, so HOW can you receive Peer Gynt notices, you foolish child. It's enough that you miraculously hold and charm the audience throughout – no other actor in England could do this; but it's NOT a career builder and you CAN'T get notices comparable to a classical role. Mantovani can't be discussed on the same level as Heifetz, because his choice of music isn't sufficiently deep and profound and reverberating. The notices on the whole have been *very* good for a work of this sort. It's done your career a world of good, so stop expecting great notices, if you choose non-great plays – by a *non*-skilled playwright (whatever his charm).' She was right, and having rather pettily (and probably incomprehensibly) cut Michael Coveney, whom I had known personally for many years, at the London Library, I settled down to play the part and share the show with the audiences who came; not nearly as many as might have come if the reviews had been better, but enough to make the experience joyful.

Aziz was now back in Geneva, which always troubled him. He had fashioned an existence for himself there which was somehow joyless, within the paralysing ambit of his mother; his flat, in the Vieille Ville, was small, dark, sterile, and very, very expensive, which in itself oppressed him – like the Chekhovian character that he was, he felt simultaneously guilty about his wealth and incapable of functioning without it. He had his television, his books and his films; he even had a piano, on which he doodled charmingly. Talented though he was, he would never play for more than five minutes, and never anything other than watery imitations of Michel Legrand. The room was dominated by a ceramic figure of an etiolated, wooden doll-like figure on a chair which was too large for it. 'This,' his mother had pleasantly remarked when she gave it to him, 'reminds me of you.' When he and I were together, we had fun, of course, in that room, but it was an almost guilty fun, as if we were contravening the spirit of the place. Aziz was both contented and miserable in it, cowed but safe. Sometimes he used wistfully to muse on how nice it would be if he never had to leave the room, and could have his meals delivered through a serving hatch. 'And would you call this hatch,' I inquired, 'umbilicus?' He laughed, almost affectionate towards his own condition, though he knew that it was slowly killing his capacity for life.

8

During the run of *Balthasar B*, Peggy would often drop a note and a shopping basket of presents in to the stage door; I would write a note of thanks in my dressing room and drop it off to her that night on my way home, and the next morning there would be her reply on my doorstep. I might then reply to her reply, dropping it into the street-level letterbox at Goodwin's Court that afternoon on the way to the theatre. We had many lunches, but also, increasingly, when I was free at the weekend, we would go to a concert, or simply to supper, and then back to her flat to round the evening off. Concerts were occasions of great intensity. Both Peggy and I were profoundly susceptible to the emotional power of music; its charms, far from soothing, only inflamed our savage breasts, and often we would sit side by side, shaking, fighting off sobs. I recall one concert, Mahler's 8th Symphony, at the Royal Albert Hall, when we sat in a box, Peggy in front and I behind, and all I could see for the whole of the last movement, as the tears coursed down my face, was her back shuddering uncontrollably. Mahler, as far as Peggy was concerned, was off-limits: 'far too dangerous to have in the house.' At the same time, even here she was capable of the most unexpected responses. We went to hear Giuseppe Sinopoli conduct the 5th Symphony, in his curiously detached, almost alienated, manner, reducing the usually overwhelming opening

Funeral March to a feelingless demonstration of certain interesting compositional methods. I became aware of Peggy, normally hypnotised by the musicians, fumbling for something in her bag. Finally she found what she was looking for, a pen and a piece of paper, wrote something on it, and handed it to me. 'What fun!' it said. Afterwards, I spoke with dissatisfaction of the performance. 'To think what Bruno Walter made of this music!' She reacted impatiently. 'Bruno Walter's long dead. We can't keep doing things the way Bruno Walter did.'

It was vocal music, whether in the opera house or in the concert hall, which brought forth the greatest emotion; this was not unconnected with the fact that Peggy had been a professional singer, even once singing the title rôle in *Carmen* for the Carl Rosa. 'Not a good voice,' she said, 'but a very loud one.' Once, at the Queen Elizabeth Hall, I commented on the bust of Benjamin Britten in the foyer. 'Oh yes,' she remarked casually, 'he used to accompany me before the war.' She could clearly have had a career as a singer, but I suspect that the music's emotional effect on her was too deep for comfort. Once we went to a concert in which Jessye Norman, attired in a huge tent-like garment on the front of which was Wagner, on the back Mozart, sang a group of Strauss songs with orchestra conducted by Simon Rattle, culminating in *Zueignung*. At the interval, we, who were never lost for words, fell utterly silent in the midst of a vast noisy throng at the Royal Festival Hall, unable even to catch each other's eye for fear of complete collapse.

After the concert came supper, the second part of our social ritual. The restaurant was often chosen for its ambience or associations as much as for the food; we'd often try out a new restaurant, or indeed a new cuisine, Lebanese, Turkish, Thai. Once we went to the Japanese restaurant at St James's, where Peggy assured me we would have our feet washed by geishas. This did not happen, but it was in every other regard highly successful, above all because it provoked in Peggy a flood of memories of her childhood trip to Japan with her parents. Japan and all things Japanese meant a great deal to her; she was immersed in every kind of Japanese art, and highly knowledgeable about it. But we never went back there, or to any other Japanese restaurant; the mere act of recall was often painful to Peggy, summoning up things she had been at pains to distance herself from all her life. Our usual circuit included the Café Royal, Boulestin, and L'Écu de France, as well as innumerable restaurants in the Earl's Court area, but our constant favourite, which we visited the day it opened and the day, some years later, when it closed, was Les Tourments de l'Amour in New Row, its name so deeply satisfactory to both of us. We talked about our work, about what we had seen or what we were reading. I would eat and drink huge quantities, lovingly egged on by Peggy, who only picked at her dishes, sipping a single glass of wine, which she would then push over to me, three-quarters full, at the end of the meal. I could never eat enough to satisfy her; there would be starters and main courses, desserts and cheese boards, apéritifs, wine and then Armagnac or Courvoisier. If there were chocolates to be had, chocolates too would be summoned. She loved me to smoke, cigarettes, one of which she would sometimes share, or cigars, the best the restaurant could manage. Sometimes she'd take a puff of one; it suited her wonderfully well, until she collapsed in a coughing fit.

Throughout all this process of pandering to my appetite,

she dealt with the waiters with an exquisitely sexy courtesy which had them almost literally at her knees. Whenever she entered a restaurant, she created a frisson, regardless of whether they had seen her before or knew who she was. They knew *what* she was, and that was a person of consequence. From their collective subconscious they summoned up a style of service which must have died with the Second World War, an extraordinary attentiveness, a discretion, a capacity to listen and to interpret, a bond between them and the customer, which I have never seen since or before. They were hypnotised by Peggy, and she could have anything she liked from them. Once, in Boulestin, she expressed to me a longing for one of their ash-trays; her hand fluttered lustfully over one, and I knew that in seconds it would disappear into her handbag. Bourgeois to the last, I begged her to ask a waiter if she could buy one. Indulging my absurd scruples, she called one over, and said how much she admired the ashtrays; could she perhaps – this said with an irresistibly knowing smile – give him the money for one? Within a second he had returned with four, which he begged her to take with the compliments of the management. She always overtipped ('women always do') but that was quite unconnected with the way they treated her; they recognised quality when they saw it. There was never any question in their eyes as to who was in charge. I was the escort, never the host, even when, as increasingly happened, I picked up the tab, grateful to find some way to repay her generosity. She liked this immensely, and never resisted. At such moments I became her beau.

We then took a taxi back to Earl's Court. On the strength of one of our first meetings, when I had spotted, hailed and secured a taxi in the middle of the rush hour, Peggy attributed to me legendary powers at taxi-hailing, almost always doomed to disappointment, but to the day she died, she was convinced that I was good luck when it came to taxis; as she was convinced that she was, in every other area. 'I'll bring you good luck, now that we know each other; I always do, to everyone I'm ever associated with. Not to myself, though.' When not artificially illuminated for a party, or unnaturally dark for a *souper sur l'herbe*, the flat in Redcliffe Square was revealed to be a long basement apartment consisting of a hall, two bedrooms, a box room, a front room, a bathroom, a toilet, a kitchen and a small garden. Yellows and beige determined the palette; there were prints, posters and paintings on every wall; *objets trouvés* and *objets d'art*, particularly of oriental provenance, scattered around; gewgaws, bibelots and netsuke on every available surface; lamps everywhere, to alleviate the subterranean gloom; books by the thousand; piles of records; feathers and bulrushes; the screen, collaged from a hundred feline images, that Ken Halliwell had made in his bid for artistic independence from Joe Orton; and here and there, discarded garments, either replaced for others more suitable, or simply thrown off in impatience at the very idea of wearing clothes at all. The same glamorous chaos that characterised her office prevailed here. The air, as at Goodwin's Court, was voluptuously fragrant; often the scent was of Mitsouke, Diaghilev's chosen perfume.

It quickly became an enchanted place for me. We would always enter in high spirits, switching on lights and filling the place with our presence. Once we came in to discover that an army of giant slugs had crawled in through the open French windows and made their way across the front room into the kitchen, where they were now calmly travelling up the walls and onto the ceiling. This science fiction nightmare appalled and exhilarated Peggy in equal measure, as did any untoward development. It was as if it were the end of the world, but that this was a prospect which she relished. I and the Button, summoned, in Peggy's highly idiosyncratic cat-talk which nonetheless always did the trick ('Comee-long, comee-long, wah, wah, wah'), did what we could to banish the slugs, goaded on by Peggy from a safe distance, whirling like a Dervish and waving various long wooden implements. The flat was a constant source of drama; on one occasion, the fridge failed to work so I went to investigate with a screwdriver. I slipped, and plunged the screwdriver through a pipe, causing the frozen gas within to escape with a profound sigh. Again Peggy was dismayed but awed. 'You have killed the fridge,' she said, with epic melancholy. Another time when she was on her own she had left the gas tap on in the kitchen; when she got up in the middle of the night to make a cup of tea, it exploded, hurling her tiny frame against the wall, and covering her from head to foot in bruises. She continued as if nothing had happened, showing up to work the next morning, to the horror of her staff. They begged her, as did I, to see a doctor. She refused point-blank, and sure enough, within a week, all the bruises had disappeared.

Once the drama of arrival at the flat was over – there generally was a drama of some sort – the third part of the evening would commence with feeding the Button (a curiously independent figure of, to her, fluctuating gender: 'He and I share a flat and we live our own lives. I once had a cat to whom I became *devoted*, and when I had to go on tour I had to put him in a cage at an animal shop, and I *wept* and *wept*. I can't have that kind of useless affection attached to some creature like her, who prefers to "walk by himself", like Kipling's cat'). Things would then proceed with feeding me all over again, as she plied me with yet more food – 'this lovely little Stilton I found in Hobbs' – and wine from her small but phenomenal cellar, every bottle a triumph of the vintner's art, unerringly chosen by her despite her lack of real knowledge about wine.

She had a cabinet full of exotic liqueurs, too, which she would mix together in sometimes successful combinations, and the full range of drinker's accoutrements, shakers, strainers and ice-grinders. There were more cigarette boxes everywhere, stuffed with Balkan Sobranie, or the coloured variety, Sobranie Cocktail, or Sullivan Powell's No 1 bought from their shop in the Burlington Arcade. There was the television, which was Work, and which we therefore never watched together. And there was the record player, with two large loudspeakers, an amplifier and a turntable, which must have been the *dernier cri* when Peggy's client John McGrath bought it for her, but which was now a little erratic. Not sufficiently so, however, to interfere with the ineffable pleasure that we derived from it.

Once established in our respective seats, Peggy in her armchair, me at her side, we listened, in the intensely charged silence of the night, initially to her small but select collection of records and then increasingly to the ones with which I bombarded her: singers of the past, Schumann, Lehmann, Josef Schmidt, Pertilé; orchestral music of the twentieth century, Strauss, Schoenberg, Zemlinsky (*never* to Mahler, of course); the chamber music of Schumann and Brahms; above all, Schubert's quintet for strings, played by an ensemble including Tortelier and Casals. Sometimes, as we listened, we would hold hands, but that was a little too explicit. Generally we sat in separate pools of emotion, as if contemplating some grief that was beyond physical or verbal expression, a grief that we both knew about but could not name.

Despite this underlying sadness, these nocturnal encounters were curiously elating; we touched something very deep in our inner lives, the crucial thing that we had in common, some fundamental sense of loss or deprivation that was the real source of all the energy and achieving with which we both, in our different ways, braved the world. The music spoke of this paradise lost that we were both – in our work but most particularly in our loves – trying to recreate. Before we listened to the music, we would speak, above all, of our childhoods, Peggy of her South African upbringing, I of mine in suburban South London, in the Berkshire countryside, and in Northern Rhodesia and at school in South Africa. This African connection was a strong bond between us. Peggy would beg me to affect a South African accent; when I did, she would too, shrieking with delight. When she discovered that I had gone to school in Grahamstown, in the Cape, she was moved: she had gone to University there. Our bonds of sympathy and shared experience sometimes led her to blur the differences between us: 'How extraordinary to think that we were in Grahamstown together and we didn't know each other!'

Over the years she told me the story of her early days many times; the details occasionally changed, but the essential facts remained: her Jewish family background (on her father's side); his inheritance of an already failing ostrich farm from her grandfather; his subsequent career as a military doctor; her world tour with her parents at the age of six including, unforgettably, Japan; her uncontrollable energy and sense of mischief as a girl, which led her best friend's father, a children's book writer, to pen and later publish a story about her, entitled *Naughty Peggy;* her adolescent discovery of her attractiveness to men ('they were like flies around a honey pot'). She told me about her love affair with Jascha Heifetz, then touring Africa, who had insisted that it was impossible for him to play unless she was in the audience. She thus became very familiar with the violin concerto repertory, about which she was now somewhat unenthusiastic. She had had a brief university career studying psychology; there she married her professor on his promise that he would take her to England; to let herself off the sexual hook, she had pretended to frigidity in the marriage, knowing that it would fascinate him for clinical reasons. When they returned to England, she had deserted him on arrival, getting out of the cab in St Martin's Lane on the way from the station, and never seeing him again. Then followed desperate years of poverty; a career as an opera singer, followed by another career as an actress; her management of 'Q' theatre; and finally, her establishment as a play agent. The rest was history.

We rarely talked about her work with writers, although I noted with interest that her relationship with her authors and their plays was essentially amorous. First, there was love: she fell passionately in love with their work, was obsessed by it, and them. Then, when they became clients, love turned into marriage, with all that implied. Affection would remain, interest even, but with it exasperation, frustration and something perilously close to contempt; all because the initial experience of love was somehow betrayed. That happy first emotion could sometimes return for brief unexpected periods, and then she would describe their new play or film script to me. For the most part, however, our conversation was not about them but about ourselves.

Her story was brilliantly, colourfully dramatic and she told it with considerable aplomb. What was strikingly absent from it was love. Passion was there a-plenty, of course. Her affairs were presented as imperatives, almost compulsions; each burnt themselves out and were then finished, done. Sometimes they were simply disappointing. 'Alas, I didn't love Ionesco – to me he was a sad child needing comfort and his remarks didn't bouleverse me; it was part of the child, and *touching*. My own feelings are so much *wilder*!' She had eventually found him boring. Once, she told me, he had telephoned to say that he would be arriving at Victoria Station at a certain time; could she be there to welcome him? She had agreed, but was dismayed at the prospect until, by an entirely characteristic leap of logic, she had decided that the only way to make the encounter tolerable was to disguise herself in some way. Slipping round the corner to Theatre Zoo, a theatrical costumiers in New Row, she bought herself a pig mask and then, in greatly improved spirits, took a taxi to Victoria, wearing it. As Ionesco came off the train, she greeted him – as a pig. 'Much to his credit,' Peggy reported, 'he made no comment whatever, continuing to converse quite normally. I greatly admired him for that.' No doubt for the author of *Rhinoceros*, nothing out of the ordinary had occurred; but it was the end of the affair.

There was no sense in her life of a continuity of love; no figure in it for her like my grandmother, who had drawn me to her great warm bosom during all those crucial years of infancy and childhood. Peggy held her parents and her brother in scant regard. For her mother she reserved her particular scorn: she was vain, inconsistent, pretentious. 'The thing I shall never, never forgive her for,' Peggy would say, 'is that she made out that we got our clothes at Marshall and Snelgrove, whereas actually they came from Swan and Edgar. Such a small lie, so petty. I despised her for it.' It was Peggy's mother, who, believing her husband's Jewishness to be a social drawback, changed their name from Vilenski to Venniker; this, too, Peggy found contemptible. But behind these strictures was something else, of which she spoke in a very quiet voice, one morning at two a.m. She said that she had a memory of herself, the most vivid of all her memories. She was a very little girl, three or four years old. It was raining heavily. Her mother was going away, off to some party, and Peggy was standing there at the window, down which the rain was streaming, watching her mother disappear, as tears coursed down her face, hot tears of longing and of loss. 'And I suppose I am that little girl today.' Small wonder that Proust was, in the end, for Peggy, the greatest of all writers.

It was her profound belief that our lives are set on course by the time we are seven years old. 'Oh those first seven years! And will you discover the *truth* about your mother?' she asked me when I embarked on a course of Jungian psychoanalysis, largely to try to find out more about Aziz, who was doing the same thing. 'Good lord, animals are lucky – they are born, weaned, thrown out into the world, without this *awful* hang-up, which destroys nearly everyone.' She wrote to me once about Eudora Welty: 'like Willa Cather she comes from a large country with vistas. Unlike us she has a deep, rich childhood, pervading love and care which has somehow launched her life on some rich moving stream. I think it is what she IS and her roots and love which have made her a writer . . . I don't know HOW one regulates one's life, if one has a bad destructive childhood. But one HAS to lay down a continuous inner life which runs like a dark stream in one's subterranean subconscious.' The note of loss, of grief, and of abandonment, was never far away.

By the end of one of our evenings – it might be two or even three in the morning – Peggy would go to bed with a play or two, and fall asleep reading them. The next morning, she would be up at six, to finish reading the plays, wash and dress herself, have a slice of toast and a cup of tea, write me a note, pluck a couple of flowers from the garden, walk round to my flat and deposit them on the landing inside my front door, then, as often as not, walk into the office: a good three-quarters of an hour's walk through South Kensington, across the park, and down Piccadilly. If the weather was even slightly clement, she would do so in her bare feet; she had troublesome bunions which no shoe could comfortably fit, and she preferred to go without whenever possible (her passion for going barefooted was another legacy of her South African childhood). When she got to the office, she would plunge into the day's work at full speed from the first moment. Her health seemed indestructible, though I began to be concerned about the pressure under which she lived, just as she fretted about the pressure under which I lived. 'Peggy,' I wrote to her, in a tone which I began more and more to adopt, 'I'm very WORRIED about your health – not your health as such, or even some temporary lack of it, but the way you PUSH yourself so fiercely when you're not at your own usual impossibly high levels. You must accept your body's advice and slow down a bit – at least GET SOME SLEEP. When are you going to have a holiday? Can't you bring the date forward a bit? It's your nerves that seem to be under continuous and impossible attack.' Though we shared a fascination with doctors, whom we collected like first editions (she after all was the daughter and the sister of one), she only went to them out of curiosity; her regime of vitamins and her frugal eating habits kept her in balance. Her social life was also extremely circumscribed; she didn't wear herself out on other people. During all the time we knew each other, I was her social life, in fact.

As for me, on a typical evening of ours, I would have wended a somewhat woozy way back to my flat, perhaps have listened to some more music, often even drunk a little more, ruminating on what had passed between Peggy and me that night, and finally hit the sack. I was usually alone.

9

Aziz and I were in constant contact by telephone, and began to see each other regularly, despite the show. I'd fly to him on Sunday morning, anywhere in Europe, and come back on Monday afternoon. These regular reunions were exciting, in their way, but the pressure to have a wonderful time was sometimes something of a strain. His emotional investment in them was enormous, to the degree that sometimes he'd almost burnt himself out emotionally by the time we met. Side by side with the glamorous locations, the sensational meals, the passionate reunions, almost co-existing with them, in fact, was the growing shadow of his mental condition. There was therapy, there were drugs; everything either exacerbated the condition, or induced a state of catatonia, frightening to see. While our sexual passion for each other increased, if anything – it was sometimes the only way we could communicate at all – there was a darkness on the horizon which, from being a tiny cloud, inexorably grew until it blotted out everything else.

Our closeness was unimpaired except for a couple of months in the Spring of 1982 when we parted over an absurd matter of sexual jealousy. Aziz had been on a rising curve of manic energy over the foregoing weeks, acquiring new friends and planning crazy ventures. It was good to see him so vital, though the manic phase of the cycle is almost as alienating as the depressive: there is a terrible hardness about the energy, an inability to listen or to respond which amounts to losing the person in question as completely as when depression engulfs them. He had met a young man who was terribly good-looking, and this man had become Aziz's new best friend – or rather, his new new best friend, because these friendships were being made on an hourly basis. This one was quite exceptionally handsome, a great splendid figure of a man, and when Aziz announced that they were going to go away together to Venice, all kinds of ugly emotions welled up inside me, not least the feeling that they were going to scoot off and have fun while I was toiling, night after night, in a West End Theatre, and would undoubtedly fall in love with each other, because how could two such attractive and sexy men fail to fall in love with each other in Venice of all places – and so on and so forth. It was a typically banal fit of pique. Foolishly, instead of expressing it and giving vent to a healthy tirade, I brooded on my suspicions, and when Aziz had gone back to Geneva, I determined in my heart to end our relationship. As soon as I realised that is what I wanted to do, I felt an immense relief; the thought of an end to the constant monitoring of moods, the need to be permanently on the look-out, was very sweet to me. I was extremely anxious, however, about the effect it might have on him, and so – could I really have done this? – I got in touch with his psychiatrist in Zurich and asked him whether he could take it. 'Best thing that could possibly happen to him,' said the psychiatrist, a bluff Englishman, 'make him stand on his own two feet.' And so I wrote a letter, in measured terms, more in sorrow than in anger, full of self-reproach and loving thoughts, and making him promise to call me the moment he received it. Which he did, and we had a very civilised conversation, and he went to Venice, but nothing came of it, because apart from anything else, the young man in question was rather severely heterosexual and engaged to be married, a fact I had failed to take in as I indulged so voluptuously in my righteous anger.

Peggy passionately approved of the parting, of course: 'You were brave and *right* to end this, but *never* regret it, because it gave you enormous expectation, passion, delirium and despair . . . to "feel" is everything! But to prolong and compromise – NO.' I was not so sure. I displeased Peggy greatly by telling her that I felt as if I now inhabited a black and white universe when before it had been in Technicolor. In fact, I missed him terribly, and found that I loved him more than ever. The break-up lasted three months, during which time we spoke constantly by telephone, until one day, realising that the following Sunday would be April 11th, the anniversary of our first meeting, and that I would therefore not be acting in the play that night, I said, 'We could meet, do you think it's playing with fire?' And he said, 'I think it's playing with fire. Let's play,' and a day or two later there I was being met by him at the airport, both of us terribly shy, pecking the other chastely on the cheeks, marvelling at how we'd forgotten what the other looked like – smelt like – then going back to his flat, and my feeling almost suffocated, suggesting we go out for a drink, a snack, and us ending up, on the first porcelain day of spring on the tiny Île Rousseau, Lac Leman at our feet, the still snow-laden mountains behind us, and blue, blue skies above, sipping beer, and trembling and stuttering. Finally, from the pit of my stomach the words, 'I want you so much,' welled up and he laughed for joy, never expecting to hear again the words which had been his daily tribute for so long, and we repaired to his flat and we made love. It was messy, unachieved from too much emotion, but that was nothing to us, because we had found each other again. 'What are we now?' he asked, not without anxiety, the next morning. 'Are we lovers?' 'I think you could say so,' I smiled.

Then followed the greatest flowering of our love. It was much changed from what it had been. In fact, something completely new had entered the relationship, something I did not at first understand. Peggy, always submissive in the face of genuine passion, instantly saw this, and, awed and dismayed, told me so. 'You're quite, quite different,' she said, with a sweet sadness. The next day I wrote to her. 'There is a change in the heart of the relationship and hence in me. Having passed through cauterising passion, self-denigration, loss of desire, and finally good-friend, fuck-buddy chumminess, something new has emerged. Its essential feature,' I said, 'is tenderness, transcendent tenderness. The communication is on a different plane, a different time-scale. It's hard to explain, because I suppose it's so unexpected. Seeing scalding passion as the summum bonum, I'm somewhat taken aback to find that this almost liquid state of being is the higher condition. Two people can flow into each other, streaming and brimming and trickling and paddling and every other kind of aquatic thing – not hurl themselves against each other. Love-making becomes like some unending underwater ballet. To put it another, quite different way, we have maybe entered the realm where, say, an actor becomes an artist. The realm, yes, I have to say it, and don't know what I'm saying, but know that I'm right, of the soul. The funny thing is, it's almost impersonal – yes, of course I "love" him, and his body, but I can't explain this, what's happening now, in terms of either his body or his mind or his personality. If all this is incoherent, it's because I'm rather fazed by it all.' I now realised, I told Peggy, that love was not a state, not an emotion, but a place, a location: a plateau, perhaps, an elevated place of safety. Almost impatiently, Peggy wrote back to me: 'Dearest Child – But what you are talking about is LOVE – *which is impersonal* and which is the ultimate gift life bestows on us, and touches the "soul" because it isn't grasping, or greedy, wishing to "possess" someone and to come. Part of it is compassion and tenderness and sadness, which is missing from passion *alone*, which is an exploration of the senses alone and is a "conquering" thing and therefore has its basis in selfishness.'

Aziz and I now cleaved together more and more intensely, despite the profound imbalance in our situations, I becoming ever more energetic and effective in the world, he fading and shadowy. Our love for each other had indeed changed. If I had once felt an imbalance in our commitment, that was no longer the case. He now gave himself to me absolutely, freely admitting that he needed me. I was essential to his life. I was his life. And yet he had no real part in my life. Not merely the enforced geographical separation, but also his fundamental inability to pursue an occupation, made him, like a Turgenev character, 'a superfluous man'. He could find no role in my life; he didn't know how to cook, or to clean, or even to answer the telephone. Nor did I want him to do any of these things. I wanted him to be my partner, my equal. Sometimes he would sigh, and say: 'if we were in Hollywood and I was a girl, I could just be your wife or your mistress. Nothing else would be expected of me.' Ever since I knew him, he had been obsessed with Audrey Hepburn. Half-humorously, he would take her pose from *Breakfast at Tiffany's:* 'how do I look?' he would say, imitating her odd Anglo-Dutch rising inflection. As time went on, he seemed to be concentrating on being her, languid, fragile, exquisite. He seemed wholly to have abandoned any thought of making movies himself. There had been a time when he had felt that he had a unique talent – a tiny one, he used disparagingly to say, but one which made a statement all his own. Now he found that statement sterile. Its elliptical, hermetic cleverness had come to seem to him emblematic of his own condition, and he could see no way out of it. There were no other stories he wanted, or knew how, to tell, and he fell into a sort of paralysis.

Then, at a certain point, an extraordinary change came over him. A friend of a friend – an actor – recommended a doctor who was prescribing anti-depressants. He gave some to Aziz, and, in conjunction with the strictly contra-indicated Carlsberg Special that he continued to drink compulsively, within 24 hours he went roaring to the top of the manic-depressive cycle. It was both exhilarating and terrifying. 'Az is whizzing around going to movies and plays and so on with his friends,' I wrote to Peggy. 'He's very high, a little mad, wildly in love with life (and me, it has to be said), writing a play, planning screenplays, doing prodigies around the flat.' One night he had painted all the furniture green; another day there were red cushions everywhere made by him, held together not by cotton thread but by glue. 'It's somewhat exhausting and a little alienating. He's desperate for my approval, my endorsement. I just say, get on with it, it's your life, be who you are, make your mistakes, create your kingdom. It's very extraordinary: the birth of a personality, really, nothing less. I suppose that's what it amounts to. He's never severed the umbilicus. Now I think he can. He says to me, Promise, promise you won't leave me till I'm ready to stand on my own feet. I assure him that I've no intention of doing so. But it sure is a different ball game from the one we started playing a couple of Aprils ago . . . ' One night, when *The Beastly Beatitudes of Balthasar B* was going through one of its many rough patches, we experienced an unusually good house, most welcome, a shower in the desert. Aziz was at the performance that night, and at the end of the show, he arrived in my dressing room, oddly nervous. 'You mustn't be angry,' he said, 'but I have a little surprise for you. Come upstairs to the bar.' I went up with the utmost apprehension, amply fulfilled when I turned the corner to see a hundred of my best friends with glasses in their hands all beaming from ear to ear. Aziz had bought the whole of the stalls for that night and secretly arranged this extraordinary event over the past couple of weeks. It was a wonderful thing to have done, and a terrible one, generous, reckless and on a massive scale (it must have cost him a fortune), and at the same time inappropriate (what were we celebrating?), embarrassing and somehow – I blushingly felt – unprofessional. To have your boyfriend buy sackfuls of tickets for your flagging show is a little humiliating. And yet he meant it so well. It was something he could do for me, a great flamboyant, theatrical gesture of love.

I hardly knew how to respond. There was an agonising moment as I hovered at the door of the bar, my face locked in a grinning rictus, but the agony soon dissolved in the good fellowship of our chums and in the champagne which Aziz had so plentifully laid on, and no more was said on either side until I had thanked him as lovingly as I knew how. Peggy, who had not been there, was appalled, and, unmoved by the depth of his despair, continued unyieldingly in her letters: 'Oh LORD how unhappy we make *ourselves* and we don't grasp the *wonders* of living! To be alive is *amazing*. Aziz must love you, and stop dramatising this feeling and modelling his *present* feelings on yours of last year (which were *mad* but FELT). Whereas his are really false . . . when one feels, one tries to hide it and be brave – and he must BEHAVE. You gave him yourself and all your passion – isn't that enough? Must he yelp for MORE – it's his, always, and no one can take it away from him . . . yes we must love and feel, but not dramatise things to falseness or absurdity. One must ENDURE, and go *through* pain and anguish and, as Gide says, if one does not flinch, and one lets misery envelop one, one arrives at the other side.' She could only see his elation as false, a projection of his lack of personal resolve. Of course, his state of driven emotional exuberance could not last. The doctor realised what he was doing and strictly prohibited him from drinking Carlsberg. He immediately declined into mild depression, exacerbated by nostalgia for his former condition. It began to be hard for him to make conversation, and when he did, he lamented the disappointment he felt I must be experiencing. No assurance of mine would convince him to the contrary, and he returned to Geneva almost with relief. We resumed our telephonic relationship, always intense, often very sexy, and our intercontinental rendezvous, which, again, were full of tenderness and passion, but increasingly silent, shadowed by the sense of doom with which Aziz was now almost always dogged. Only in the act of love were we able to lose the sense of insoluble difficulties bearing down on us

inexorably. Then we truly lost ourselves in ecstatic oblivion, expanding through time and space into a place where
the world was left a very long way behind.

Meanwhile Peggy and I, in what in retrospect seem to be
obscenely high spirits by contrast, had started work on our
most intense collaboration, my first book.

10

The idea that I might write a book at all was hers. I had never dared to dream of such a thing, though to be a writer was my first identified ambition and remained my secret hope. In fact, my very first published writing, for the London Evening Standard, owed a great deal to Peggy, and what she taught me on that occasion has informed everything I have ever written since. It was an article about the show in which I was then appearing, *The Beastly Beatitudes of Balthasar B*, and I determined that the piece would be a masterpiece of wit and style, and so it was, I felt, after many hours of toil, and having filled many wastepaper baskets with discarded drafts. My satisfaction with the piece began to waver somewhat as I trudged up the stairs at Goodwin's Court, and disappeared entirely as she took the piece and, in that alarming gesture of hers, closed her fist over the arm of her spectacles, removed them, and applied her face to the text. I had met Peggy's writers in the street, on their way to the office with their latest manuscript. They had the air of condemned men. When Peggy judged a script, or any piece of writing, it was in a different voice from her usual one. She would suspend all sense of her personal relationship with you; the spectacles would go back on, 'Well,' she would say, and then briskly deliver the verdict. It was never qualified; the judgement was simply, as far as she was concerned, revealed truth. She was an oracle; she served strange gods. One listened. One had to. Going to see Peggy was like confession: you left your ego at the door, and. opened yourself totally to the experience. This, you thought, taking a deep breath, is going to be good for me.

This Evening Standard piece was my first experience with the oracle. Having relieved me of the crumpled pages with professional unceremoniousness, she applied herself to it. Tut-tutting the while, sighing, occasionally shouting out protests – 'dear God!' – she got to the end of the piece, put her spectacles on again and inquired pleasantly and with curiosity, 'Did you mean it to be so boring?' Without waiting for my reply, she quoted a phrase: 'You've written A bit of a Ming vase, J. P. Donleavy. What do you mean?' 'He's very delicate.' 'Have you ever seen a Ming vase? They're very sturdy, you know. It's very hard to break them.' Then she went through the text, tutting again: 'Adjectives, adjectives, adjectives,' citing a number of adverbs. 'Strange,' she said. 'You write wonderful letters to me, in your own voice. Why are you writing in this strained manner? Write it as if you were writing it to me. And I must see everything you write about. Make me see it.' The next day, I came back with a new piece, conversational, factual, adverb-free. No tuts, this time, no shouts or sighs. At the end she said, 'It's awfully good. Why is it so much better?' 'Guess,' I said. Then she said, 'It needs one last sentence,' which she proceeded to inscribe at the bottom of the article. It was a slightly sentimental conclusion, not quite to my taste, but of course I let it stand. When the piece was printed, the Standard cut this line. Peggy understood writing as no one else I have met has ever done, but she was not a writer – except in her letters, which are perhaps the most perfect expression of her personality.

The book – our book – had a convoluted origin. It started as a lecture I was invited to give at Goldsmiths' College towards the end of 1981. I imagine they expected a sort of chat about the stars – what's Felicity Kendal really like? How do you learn the lines? and so on – but I determined instead to sum up, magisterially, everything I had discovered about the job in the ten years during which I had practised it. When I came to deliver the lecture, there were about twenty people in the rather large auditorium, among whom was a mysterious, curiously restless woman swathed in diaphanous scarves: Peggy, disguised as herself. I only managed to deliver a third of what I had to say in the allotted time; even if I had ever got to the end, I suspect that my remarks might have seemed somewhat opaque. I wanted to write a philosophical and literary masterpiece, intellectually profound and verbally inspired; but the result, which I had planned to call – after Brecht – *The Little Organon on Acting*, was, despite a few decent jokes and a couple of accurate observations, confusing and pretentious. Peggy was sweet about it, but fairly non-committal. However, when I met an editor of the New York Times at a lunch party, and she said that she was looking for an article by an actor, I suggested to Peggy that we might yet carve something out of it, and gave her the Goldsmiths' text. 'Your article: in a way it's not *absolutely* ideal for the New York Times,' she wrote. 'It's absolutely sweet but not quite sufficient, sophisticated enough – it slightly underrates the readership and treats them like students. But let's cut it up and see.' Then she had a new idea. '*Certainly* Methuen would publish THIS, as it's ideal for the young and for students.' She had it typed up and sent it to Nick Hern, publisher of the most influential list in the world of theatre publishing. Meanwhile,

The Beastly Beatitudes of Balthasar B having come to a long overdue end, in June of 1982 I went to Santa Fe for four weeks with the National Theatre as part of the British American Theatre Institute, not only to act but also to teach and direct, and under the intoxicating impact of these new activities (not to mention the dry red beauty of New Mexico itself), I rather forgot about the article and its fate.

As if with heavy symbolism, the night I arrived I witnessed a total eclipse of the moon – 'like a slow shutter on some great camera,' I wrote to Peggy – and I knew that nothing would ever be the same again for me; it was a watershed. The place and what I did there conspired to turn my expectations of life upside down. 'To come back from Santa Fe much the way one arrived in it would be absurd. Change is not in question. All that is in question is the degree, and the nature, of the change. – Love from the flowering desert.' It was at the end of our time there that I got Peggy's letter telling me that Methuen had decided to advance me £1,000 to write a book based on the paper I had delivered at Goldsmiths'. Writing was my life's ambition; long before acting. Now I had a subject, and a great deal to say about it, and I could scarcely wait to start. My last few days in Santa Fe, though filled with excitement – the showing of the scenes that I had directed, the plans to return at the head of a company made up of my students, financed by a local millionaire, the farewell flight in a balloon over Albuquerque – were all secondary to my yearning to start making sentences and paragraphs and chapters and to end up with A Book. 'Don't hurry with it,' wrote Peggy; 'begin to expand it out on your return.' A vain injunction; I was incapable of proceeding decorously. I bought a massive, cumbersome electric typewriter the moment I was back in

England and set off for Geneva to meet Aziz. We would find a chalet somewhere and write: me to Methuen's commission, him to finish a screenplay that he'd long planned. And so we settled into a vast and unexpectedly cheap villa at La Claie-aux-Moines, outside Lausanne, and, to the clank of cow-bells, with Heidi's landscape stretching out before us on all sides, we wrote.

It seemed as if I would never stop. I sat at my desk at eight in the morning and could scarcely be pulled away for meals. I wrote so fast and furiously that I broke the typewriter and had to borrow a neighbour's. 'I clocked up 12,000 words today,' I wrote to Peggy. 'Of course, I know that only about half of that, if I'm very lucky, will be usable; but the flow has never stopped for a moment. I don't quite know what form it's taking; it seems to be finding its own shape. The dangers of on the one hand anecdotage and on the other sententiousness are ever-present. One thing I do know, though, Peggy, is that I'm writing well. No adjectives! It's clear, simple and accurate. Very personal, too. Maybe too much so. I'm mindful of Nick Hern's comment about the ego-trip: but the whole point of it was to try to pin down what actually does go on inside an actor.' I realised very early on that I was going to have to expose myself on many levels. 'I'm just about to come up to the section about Gay Sweatshop,' I wrote to her. 'A dilemma: how can I honestly and truly describe it and what it meant to me without acknowledging my proclivities? Yes, of course I can, but I'm so sick of the duplicity, passing for straight. I'll write it and then you can decide. It's so strange to be summing up at the age of 33. I feel as if it were a farewell to acting.'

As I wrote, the form of the book began to crystallise in my mind: I understood that my aim in writing it must be much more modest than the grandiose aspirations of the Goldsmiths' lecture. Everything in it, I saw in a sort of blinding flash, must answer the question 'What's it like being an actor?' And that – in another celestial illumination, as I thought – gave me my title. 'Does the title *Being an Actor* have any merit?' I wrote to ask Peggy. 'At first I thought it was too bald, but I've rather come to like it. It has a resonance which I can't explain.' I could, but I was shy to try: being and acting seemed almost oppositions, and I liked the tension of combining them in a sentence. Peggy was not so sure. 'What about "Becoming an Actor" (or is your "being" better). I like the *movement* of "becoming".' I knew, too, that the book must be in two halves: one half, my life as an actor, the second everyone's life as an actor: specific and then general. For the first time in my writing I tasted the incomparable thrill of experiencing the emergence of form out of incoherent matter. I had never known excitement like it.

Aziz started well, too, but then, daunted, I suppose, by sharing a room with this writing fanatic, this write-oholic, he abandoned what was a very promising, riddling, sardonic murder story in which a crazed movie fanatic kills someone who won't stop talking in the cinema, and started to go back and forth to Geneva to deal with some of the never-ending complications of his financial situation, leaving me alone tapping obsessively in the middle of the pitch-black Swiss countryside. I felt guilty. But I could do no other. I was completely gripped by my compulsion.

'What you said eighteen months ago remains as true now,' I wrote to Peggy, 'my expansiveness crushes his spirit. No wonder – along I come with my commission and my electric typewriter and sit down and spin off words from morning to night. Never mind what the quality of it is (he hasn't read any of it; but then neither have I, and shan't till I've completed one entire draft). If one has anxiety about one's creativity, it'll be doubled by all that going on in the room next door. So there is that between us. Otherwise, it's been idyllic, laughing and fooling around, going for walks, combing the area for restaurants, and being very lively in the bedroom. He is, as always, fantastically generous. If only . . . if only I could see a way to break the spell of self-limitation. He knows that that's what he's doing to himself. Essentially, however graceful and funny and loving, he behaves like a child, unable to stick at anything for more than a few minutes, requiring constant diversion, eating the oddest things in great quantity and refusing everything else.'

I came back and forth to Britain to make television pro-grammes, including a sitcom called *A Chance in a Million*, which had a certain cult success in the mid-eighties; but now I was a Writer, and not a day passed without my spending at least an hour or two at a typewriter, of which I started to collect many, electric, non-electric, portable, permanent. I reported my progress to Peggy from Spain, from France, from all the exotic places in which Aziz and I would meet for a week or even a day. She was torn between encouraging me to write – 'TAKE CARE – yes, TRY and write, though I know the lure of *living* comes between you and the page' – and urging me to slow down – 'Don't fly madly into the writing – take what time (and inclination) you have – DON'T FORCE it or rush it. There ISN'T a deadline. SO DON'T RUSH.' Finally, having read most of the book to Aziz in Venice over breakfast and lunch and supper and in the bathroom and in the bedroom and in the hall, I delivered it to Peggy in instalments and she reported on her feelings as she went through it. 'I'm on Titus – I'm in love with the WORK part of the book . . . Joint Stock etc – I HATE the excitement (and you and Ken Campbell – oh that Reich!!).' Ken had encouraged me to write a play about Wilhelm Reich which somehow never happened. 'This book would have been a Reich if I hadn't forced a commission and bullied you.' Then we hit a rock. 'But we must curtail the domestic and no theory waffling about the "problem" of homosexuality in a vacuum. THERE IS NO PROBLEM – IS THERE? – don't write in a vacuum.'

The question of whether I should refer to my homo-sexuality in the book became something of a sticking point between us. I didn't see how I could even begin to write about myself honestly as an actor without referring to it. At the most obvious level, how could I write about working for Gay Sweatshop, one of the most important events in my career, and indeed in my life? But equally how could I write about any of it, of the day to day influence of my intimate life on my work, without saying that I was gay? To Peggy it was whining, special pleading, saying 'Poor Little Me,' which was the last thing I meant it to be. 'I think it's awfully wrong to write that page about your queerness,' she remonstrated. 'The thing you praise most in Martin's play (*Passing By*) is that the guys are *accepted* as lovers and not *talked about* – to go into a discussion of "queerness" and quote people seems to me to reduce your book. In the theatre where one *acts* and doesn't *talk about it*. How will you ever get this accepted if you people push explanations and defences on us!' I simply wanted to acknowledge that quite a number of actors were gay, though perhaps not quite as many as in the popular imagination, and that they led perfectly normal lives, professionally and personally. It seemed to me important that someone with a mainstream career should say quite clearly that he or she was gay. As far as I knew, no one had yet done so. Perhaps they had tried but failed. I had told various journalists in the course of interviews that I was gay, but they would never print it: they didn't want to be told, they wanted to find out. If there was no exposé, there was no story. I was not unaware that coming out in print like this might have terrible effects on my career (though since nobody had done so, it was hard to know); but thinking that thought was enough to convince me that I must. Neither I nor anybody else should live in that sort of dread. This cut no ice with Peggy. 'I would have preferred for you to at least have removed the "of course I suppose I will never get another job" – i.e. *See how brave I am to write this, and poor little me – I'm probably going to have to sacrifice my career for my bravery* (whining)?' And of course she was right; the less fuss I made of it, the better. So I cut the out-er than thou stuff. Still she didn't really like it. This dispute rumbled on for some time.

When I had delivered both parts of the book, the section outlining my career and the one describing an actor's life-cycle from unemployment and back again, we sat down at Redcliffe Square with a bottle or two of wine and went through it, or as much of it as we could in an evening, because I argued every point that she made with what I realised must have been unusual tenacity. She was not accustomed to such resistance. I was quite clear about what I had written and why, and was not keen to change anything without good reason. Her general view was that the first section (the personal section) was good and lively but that the second section (the general account of actors' lives) was boring and ordinary: actors knew it all already, and non-actors would simply find it dull. I prayed to God that she wasn't right and filibustered, playfully, quibbling in detail over each of her observations. Finally I retired for the night and wrote to her the next day: 'Last night (Mon) was a riot. Should we just give it to N Hern as it stands and get his general reaction?' This provoked a huge storm: 'I was surprised and upset at your card saying "let's give it to Nick Hern *as it stands* and get his general reaction". (Is that how you treat your audience?) Were you suggesting that I pass on to him your congested, single-spaced, overcrowded and unrevised ms *as it stands*? Didn't you even listen when I said it *had* to be re-typed double-spaced like every ms? (You aren't in the Proust class, if we consider *revising*, alone.) Nick isn't a kind of hack, to read your 130 pages for "his general reaction" . . . You were *commissioned* to write a book by a leading publisher (Arden, Brecht, Weiss, Pinter and Bond and nearly every famous name in the theatre are published by him). He is *twenty* times busier than you are AT HIS JOB. It's so careless and arrogant – unthinking to just shove it over for "general reaction": and UNPROFESSIONAL. I read it very hurriedly but gave up HOURS between my work to do so. All you wanted to hear was that it was intensely interesting – you didn't want to hear anything else. (It was my fault that I was too tired to use that evening we had together when we just flipped through it.)'

She arranged for a typist to put it into readable shape. 'As the ms will now be well over two hundred and fifty pages and two copies should be made it's going to cost about £200 to be fit to send to Nick and it would have been nice not to waste the money on an obviously totally unrevised ms. I delivered the ms to the typist myself (5th floor, no lift). But just forget it – I'll collect the double-spaced copies and get a copy to Nick as a submitted ms. (I should point out that this isn't an Agent's job (arranging typed copies) – my playwrights simply don't behave in this way thank God!)' Curiously, I was undaunted by any of this. I also quietly believed that the book, give or take a re-write or two, was close to its final form. The experience of writing it had been exceptionally instructive; I learned to know when I was writing what I wanted to write, in the way that I wanted to write it. Whether anyone else wanted to read it or liked it was another matter, but this trust in myself as a writer was quite new; I now felt as confident in my judgement of my own writing as I did of my own acting. This personal breakthrough brought a considerable change, not only in my own self-respect generally, but in my relationship with Peggy. I had assumed an attitude of absolute deference to her judgement, especially in the arena of writing, but now I had a sort of inner certainty which immediately manifested itself in the letters that I wrote to her. I stood taller now, and there was a shift in the balance of power in our friendship.

I think Peggy was a little taken aback about my firmness of purpose. 'You were so marvellous to do the book, so much superhuman effort and so much that is splendid. Then you come back and TAIL-WAG all over town leaving me as kennel-maid!' She returned to the fray a day later. 'Don't think you've been let off. I've only read the ms once, very quickly, and as soon as you give me the small re-writes I shall read the whole book – THIS WEEKEND, please. I can see you are going to be very stubborn about cuts – we can do the next step of double spacing ms, but you WILL FIND the Methuen editing *very* tough. This is only the beginning so be as hard on yourself as you would be to others. I intend to read and mark ALL less good parts! We will have another session next week.' We didn't. I don't think it had gone at all the way she had expected.

There was one matter, however, in which I deferred to her instantly; she was so obviously right. I had started the book with a potted history of my family. Both she and Nick felt that this was a terrible turn-off; Nick felt that it should start with the sentence which began the second chapter – 'I wrote to Laurence Olivier' – and this was brilliantly correct, and gave the book the best possible opening. But even more importantly she gave me a sterling piece of advice, repeating even more forcefully what she had told me when I wrote the article for the Evening Standard: 'there is a *visual* starvation – only tiny though, but I want to actually KNOW what part of London your digs were in during the Drama School period, when you hadn't enough to eat. We need to *see* you at the NT and where you journey back each night. I also want to know what *kind* of building you trained in – was it a house? In what area? Did it have an actual stage? The theatre part keeps missing out tiny points of this kind. And we need to know just a sentence more about your Dad disappearing and where your Mum was staying through all this, that is if you want us to know. But I do feel a bit blind as I read the text – blind because I don't know how to follow you. Odd, isn't it.'

I re-wrote the manuscript from top to bottom on the strength of this. Generally it consisted of a detail here or there, but it transformed the book. It was her constant injunction to make her see what I was writing about that gives the book whatever actuality it may possess. The form was my own, and, interestingly enough, she was less taken by the sections that describe the day-to-day life of the profession, than with my reminiscences of my own career. 'In some respects the material isn't quite enough. I mean of the Joint Stock, *Amadeus* character. And I do, in some ways, think it's two different books . . . but only NICK will know this. Maybe he envisaged a book for his "Educational Series" and some of the best material transcends this. Let's see, we shall have to wait a couple of months as Nick reads interminably. But it's wonderful that you've put down so much. It's not like the reminiscences of old stars like Gielgud and Olivier, who pour out reams of 1920s gossip! I want you to be PROUD of your book, little Pup.'

Methuen accepted it. 'Animal, Canine Species!' she wrote to me triumphantly, 'Nick H has accepted "A Dog's Life in the Theatre". He says *the ancestors* are OUT. (Didn't I tell you? You can use it for another time.) I think he will use ALL Part 2.' Once Nick had approved of it, her anxieties disappeared and she began to be very fond of the book. 'You have made me fall in love with the theatre again,' she said. It was our venture, a monument to our friendship, and I dedicated it to her; a joint dedication with my grandmother: 'For Peggy, without whom this book would never have been written, and my grandmother, Vera Guise, without whom there would have been nothing to write about.' She wrote to me , 'I peeked at your ms and am hugely proud to be linked with your grandmother. You will be the third author to give me a dedication: Joe ("Loot"); Chris, and the Pup.' The one blot in all this rejoicing was the cover. I had suggested to Aziz, who had made a number of rather successful collages, that he might try one for the cover. He was galvanised by the request. The work needed to be done very quickly, so I Fedexed over to Geneva a quantity of photographs of several of the roles I had played, with the idea of demonstrating one of the themes of the book, that an actor was a sort of a professional multiphrenic. He responded very quickly and very skilfully and Nick Hern and the art department at Methuen were impressed and delighted. Not so Peggy. 'I don't think I like that collage: I don't like the dominance of that terrifying Robespierre character. Why not the sweet little face you had blown up in the centre? I don't think I like the collage at all, unless the book has some special picture as well. Actually the collage balance is very ugly and I'm sure a professional could do it better. I greatly admire Ziz's pictures but in this case I feel he has done the book and you a disservice. Maybe I'm wrong. But the collage somehow frightens me – it's so ugly.' It was certainly very forceful, which is what made it so effective; but that, it was perfectly clear, was not the primary reason for Peggy's objection. She didn't want Aziz to share in a book that belonged to us. It was as simple as that.

11

After a long period out of England, Aziz decided to come back for a short stay when I was about to open in *The Relapse* at the Lyric Theatre in Hammersmith, some two years after *The Beastly Beatitudes of Balthasar B.* He was sweet and quietly charming, but very minor key, swathed about with sadness, somehow distant, not so much in his manner as in spirit. He seemed faded, like a fabric over-exposed to the light. 'We passed a hazy happy day,' I wrote to Peggy the day he arrived back. 'Since then, he's been in a bit of a trance. Overwhelmed by being at a first night of mine again after all these years, overwhelmed to be in the flat again, overwhelmed at how it's changed. We had lunch today with my aunt and mother – which is the definition of overwhelming. He's sleeping it off at the moment. He can't face his friends here, much as he wants to see them, because they've got so much to show for the time since he last saw them – scripts, films, children – and he has nothing. He's at a standstill.' New drugs (lithium) had finally stabilised him, but the stability they brought bored him. He was not even interestingly neurotic to himself any more. His life, up till now a helter-skelter ride between heaven and hell, had become very flat, and he went back to Geneva to resume a life which consisted of visits to the psychoanalyst, to the cinema, and to certain rather miserable clubs where, very late at night and under the influence of enough Carlsberg Special, he would rediscover some of the teasing, suggestive vivacity which had so characterised him in the past. At such times, he managed, for a brief while, to find himself interesting, but by morning, this proved unsustainable. Most of his days were spent recording and painstakingly editing together on video his matchless collection of cartoons. It was the only genre with which he now seemed comfortable, scrutinising the adventures of its anthropomorphic heroes, its cunning mice, fiendish cats, cheeky rabbits and gun-toting dogs with intense concentration, as if the clue to his existence lay in these stories. Sometimes, on my visits to Geneva, we would watch them together, and these were times of great closeness, but we never said anything about them, not a word.

At the beginning of 1984, I started rehearsing Edgar Wallace's *On the Spot* at the Watford Palace Theatre, translating my admiration for Charles Laughton into a misguided desire to play one of his most famous stage roles, Tony Perelli, openly based on Al Capone. Peggy was astonished that I should want to play such an old war-horse, and gravely warned me, not for the first time, that 'you can never be better than your play,' a fundamental tenet of hers, which if not absolutely true, certainly proved to be the case here. Laughton was better than the play, and had electrified his audiences by taking every blood-thirsty line deeply seriously. He seemed to release in himself a limitless quantity of the inky fluid of murderous villainy that alone would make the play live. I strove to identify in myself a reservoir of the same substance, but could locate at most a thimbleful. 'It's not really a part of myself that I have easy access to,' I wrote to Peggy. 'I didn't quite get hold of it in

Total Eclipse, as Hare pointed out.' (He had said: 'You don't understand about the dark, do you?') 'For some reason I find myself homing in on the innocence in almost any character I play,' I continued to Peggy. 'Capone had precious little of that.'

Desperately I tried to identify his motives. 'The point about Perelli is that *he has no heart*,' Peggy wrote to me. 'Down there it is black, black, black, like a dungeon – you can't fit that into motives – it's worse – *motiveless*.' What I imagined would be a banquet of acting turned to ashes in my mouth. For the only time in my career, I took the character and his life home with me. In my nightly calls to Geneva I was aware that I was no sort of a tonic to Aziz, who was beginning to be embarrassed by his lack of anything to report about his life, external or internal: it was more of the same, and what there was, was grey. My moody obsession with Perelli brought no help. To compound the general gloom, at the end of one of her letters around this time Peggy wrote: 'I have a *bump* over my left breast, just below the neckline – hope it's a gland! Please don't talk about this to anyone, or it will get round town that I've got cancer.' Obsessed by the play, I was nonetheless immediately alarmed. 'Friday's run was fluent but empty. Unless we (and the audience) believe that the characters live in the shadow of death at every moment of their lives, we're wasting everyone's time,' I wrote, inadvertently articulating the frightening threat which seemed to be very close to our own lives. 'Now: most important: please phone me and leave a message (I'm out 14 hours a day this week) to tell me what Dr Austin said about your little gland. *I want to know.*'

Aziz arrived a few days in advance of the first night of *On the Spot;* the Sunday before, I was appearing in the Royal

Variety Performance to which, with exquisite grace and charm despite the inner despair which was all too visible to me, he escorted my mother and my aunt. He was the first of my lovers whom they had met, and their initial resistance to the very idea of acknowledging his existence melted away in the face of his winning combination of vulnerability and exotically perfect manners. They had immediately recognised the fragility of his being and after meeting him had unexpectedly and uncharacteristically expressed a strong desire to hug him; he and my grandmother had had an intense rapport, and her death eighteen months earlier had devastated him. That was in the winter of 1982, when one death succeeded another in rapid succession: first my grandmother, then a cheerful lad I'd known for years who set fire to himself in a railway sidings; a third hanged himself in despair at what he perceived to be the loss of his youthful beauty. The desperate darkness of that time was in the air again, in Aziz's condition, in the threat of Peggy's illness, in the play. 'Quel cauchemar!' I wrote after the First Night. 'But it's over now, the worst of it: press is OK, we should be able to get it right, now. Bit of a mess, I'm afraid; lot of bad acting, too. It does work, though. Playing Tony is without joy: the play (as you implied) has no humanity; no real juice. It gives one nothing. So it's hard, hard work.'

Aziz was terribly winded by the play; it upset him more than I thought possible. We avoided the subject till we were alone together in bed when he looked at me very deeply and said 'I feel as if you're a stranger. Was that you? It must have been, up to a point, or you couldn't have done it. I was terrified, really terrified, by what I saw.' I laughed and tried to prove that I was just pretending, only acting, but it was hard to dispel the mood of desolation. It was as if a betrayal

121

had occurred, a betrayal, perhaps, of innocence. A gulf of incomprehension opened up between us which could scarcely have been greater, it seemed, if I had actually committed the crimes of which my character was guilty. A little pleasure was generated by my handing him an advance copy of *Being an Actor*, with his jacket, fiercely dynamic with its overlapping black and white images of my career. I took a photograph of him, waggishly pointing at the collage he had so strikingly designed. Over supper and walking about in the streets we recovered some of the light-heartedness, a touch of the playfulness, that was more usual between us, but when Aziz went back to Geneva a few days later, things were still on an unresolved note. Meanwhile, the results of Peggy's breast cancer tests proved negative: she had to go in for what we both pretended was 'a tiny little op', but which at her age was a grave undertaking. With strained cheerfulness, I sent her off to hospital with a package of cassettes. 'These are strictly divided into pre- and post-op: Brahms and Elena Gerhardt pre-; harp and flute music post-; after a while, very gently, a little Mozart: a movement at a time. Go especially carefully with the slow movements: the Surgeon-General has determined that they may seriously damage your health.' She refused to be visited by anyone.

On the Spot continued its gory if sparsely attended course at Watford. I spoke to Aziz several times, but was unable for a few days to get hold of him. I assumed, and hoped, that he was out somewhere having a good time. Then one night a couple of weeks into the run I came home in the small hours of the morning, having had a very alcoholic post-show supper with a terribly handsome and flirtatious young man, and after leaving him slightly guiltily, I just about managed to operate my answering machine to hear a message from Aziz's brother Ahmed asking me to call him. Was Ahmed in London? I wondered. Why? It was obviously too late to call him. I went to bed and fell into a profound boozy sleep. The following morning, I struggled to my feet to see that there was another message on the machine. This was from Aziz's neighbour, Mason, an old and close friend of his, an American, and he reported, with trembling voice, that he had been told not to call me but he felt I had to know: Aziz had killed himself, it was a terrible thing, but I must be glad; he was happier now.

12

What followed hardly bears describing. Snotty and red-eyed with ugly futile mourning, still in my dressing gown, I reached for music and found the slow movement of a Prokofiev concerto, music I had once heard with Aziz, piercingly sweet against a quirky pock-pock-pock accompaniment, and I played it over and over and over again, howling and sobbing along with the soaring solo line which seemed to represent everything which was beautiful about Aziz. Unable to be still for a second, I paced up and down, suddenly sitting on the floor or the stairs, wanting to do damage to something or someone – myself, above all. I pulled out some of the hundreds of photographs I had taken of him. I hugged his non-existent form in my arms and whispered soothing words of pity to his absent self. I had the taste of him in my mouth, and that above all, pungent and inimitable, was threatening to drive me insane. The thing that saved my reason was the show: I had a show to give that night. There was no understudy, of course. Everyone that needed to be told was told; the management laid on a limousine, which, embroiled in rush hour traffic, took ten times as long to get to the theatre as a train would have done, and I arrived in a state in which eventually hysteria had given way to an other-wordliness, there but not there. The show was done, and done adequately, and my old friend the show's producer took me out for supper afterwards, fearing for me if I were to be left alone, and we talked and talked. I wept and laughed and then went home and slept suddenly and deeply and the following day experienced the first of many, many terrible mornings of waking up and remembering, and lying motionless, numb, paralysed by reality, until the grief rose up slowly and faintly, as if from a far faraway place, and finally broke in convulsive sobs.

Thereafter, the days were filled with telling his friends and mine what had happened. They already knew, of course; such news seems to pass round almost before it's happened, but they needed to hear it from me, and I needed to tell it to them, to relive it over and over, trying vainly to shape it into a meaningful narrative. Sometimes when friends came to see the show, I had to tell them then, after the hugs and the congratulations. The weeks of the run at Watford went by somnambulistically, the darkly violent play and the sleepless nights and the desperate dawns merging with the daily and sometimes twice-daily recitation of the ghastly events. I now knew more about them, from Ahmed and from Mason, who came to London to fill me in on the grim timetable of Aziz's death and to describe to me in the terrible detail I craved the circumstances of the discovery of the body. This had taken place three days – three days during which I was phoning and smiling to think of the nice time he was having – after Aziz had administered the cocktail of drugs whose recipe he had so carefully sought out and which he had so faithfully and effectively followed. Mason described in harrowingly precise terms what he had found when he burst the door open and for a week after I could see nothing but that whenever I closed my eyes. Having found out what exactly had happened, I had to try find out – not why; I suppose I knew the answer to that – then why at that precise moment.

Martin Sherman and two other friends had stayed with him in Geneva just a short time before he died, and had found him cheerful, or at least attempting to be cheerful. Mason told me that in fact he had been wearily aware of another dark tide of depression welling up, ready to engulf him, and was simply exhausted by the thought of it. The drugs prescribed by his doctor had eliminated the highs and normalised the lows, though the cycle carried on remorselessly in a subterranean sort of way, just below the surface. He was left stranded on the beach of stability, denied the dangerous thrill of surfing on the big waves of emotion, instead condemned to wait passively while the ever-encroaching tide of depression lapped around his ankles. Knowing that it would eventually recede was small consolation. He decided to put an end to the cycle, and had methodically and calmly taken the necessary steps. In the flat he had left a letter in which he divided up his wealth among his friends. In fact, he had no money of his own; it was all his family's, and they were in no position to pay out Aziz's little presents to the people he loved. To each of us he left a message. Mine was: 'Tell Simon I love him and I'm sorry. He owes me nothing.'

Guilt, rage, regret, despair tailed me, day in and day out. It was some days before I told Peggy what had happened, and I broke it to her very gently, weak as she was from her surgery; she had just come out of hospital. She fell silent, nothing left in her to deal with the complexity of what she felt. When she wrote to me, it was in subdued and pitiful vein. 'Dearest dearest little Mite. Don't spoil your years together by *desolatory* thoughts. Think how much you *gave* one another, and remember with love and gratitude and understanding. Ziz didn't WANT to live – he chose *not* to.

You couldn't have done anything, and indeed you *should* not have, since he simply DIDN'T WANT TO LIVE. You are so important and your work is so important, and you must *carry your torch*. Those of us near to you LOVE you. I feel incredibly sad because of the waste but I am so happy that you both experienced *so much* together. Fondest Fondest love, darling child.' Trying to find some way of averting the nausea that overcame me every time I contemplated his death, I wrote Peggy a letter in what I hoped was a stoical vein, an attempt at objectivity. 'For the first time, I know what Tragedy is: not unhappiness, not misfortune. Tragedy is the inevitable. Aziz was born to die this way. The Kingdom of death had an embassy in him. It's wrong to say he had no will: he had a will to die. Almost naughtily, like a naughty boy, he decided to do this grim deal with death. It was his little secret – sometimes he'd smile a curious little smile, a sort of moue, and his eyes would twinkle darkly: Narcissus peering into the vast black lake and seeing his own reflection. This secret was his long stop. His attitude to life was like that of a man who goes to a party somewhat reluctantly, thinking: I can always leave. Oh Peggy, Peggy, I loved him so. Whatever his limitation, however marked his brow, however little he thought himself able to love, he had a huge gift for provoking love. The love he provoked in me changed me utterly: it transformed my acting, too, it inspired me to write. All this he gave me: and now he's given me grief. He's completed my emotional education. I've grown up, Peggy. My deepest love to you, my only other teacher. Please can we meet soon.'

She wrote back in a way which oddly mingled a kind of sombre, tragic exaltation with eager involvement in day-to-day business: 'You are RIGHT to accept this whole extraordinary experience and you *are* facing it and living through and with it, as André Gide has said. It is constantly in my mind, and *so are you*, dearest child. I have not intruded, as I know you will ask if and when you want me. I'm leaving this at the stage door. Tom, Bill and I are down to see the play, but *not* coming round. Bill I think saw Laughton, so it will be interesting! We meet for lunch, formally, on Thursday – yes? Can you bear it? – *A SECRET*: BAFTA have a special award night in June – a famous Director, an international celebrity (last year Orson), and then a *working* member of the industry – and they have chosen *ME*!!! It's *disgraceful* that BAFTA awards are NEVER for authors. The director or the actors get them for the plays *written by the authors* – now the *final insult:* an *agent* gets it. Please tell NO ONE – it is the last thing I want as you know well. What super notices for the book!' *Being an Actor* had just appeared, just two weeks after Aziz died, resplendent in the jacket which he had designed. 'WILL IT SELL? How wonderful that the sonnets section is *ALL THERE* – and thank God you cut out the drooling about being a homosexual in general. Love is *where it falls*. What a wonderful beautiful and awesome experience. (Terror and beauty.)' And then she added, somewhat matter-of-factly: 'Awful I think that Ziz made his decision on the Thursday when I was having my operation – *he* should have lived, and perhaps *I* should have died. I wish I'd made a pact with him.' The day he had returned to Switzerland for the last time I had taken the last roll of film I took of him to the chemist to be developed. On the roll was the photograph of him holding the book up, pointing at the cover. It had now been returned, an image from beyond the grave. It is the saddest of photographs, almost unbearably poignant in the circumstances.

His death had a cathartic effect on Peggy, as death, especially sudden death, always did. There was something Nietzschean in her attitude; a sense of the necessary element of the tragic, necessary for our completion as human beings. For my part, I was humbled and suddenly matured by this encounter with death, the unnegotiable. A dark shape appeared on my horizon that has never since altogether gone away. I finished playing the rest of the short Watford run of *On the Spot*. The show somehow went on; I clamped down my grief. Between the end of the run there and the West End transfer, I went away for a week to Capri, and every afternoon, wandering alone and aimless over the island, at last grieved primitively, howling like an animal, till my throat was sore and I could howl no more. In the morning and at night, I sat and wrote down everything I could remember about our few years together. On the way back to London, I went to Geneva. I had been barred from Aziz's funeral by his mother, who blamed me for his death. Now I met his brother in one of the restaurants that Aziz and I had frequented, and he told me, with great emphasis, that on the contrary, as far as he was concerned I was the best thing, maybe the only good thing, that had ever happened to Aziz, which was wonderfully assuaging. Together we went to see the grave. It was a temporary affair, with a sort of makeshift cross stuck in the soil, incomprehensible, since he was Muslim, or at any rate his family were. Someone who must have known him very well had placed a Mickey Mouse among the flowers. It was 11th April 1984, exactly four years to the day since we first became lovers.

'It was on April 11th two years ago,' I wrote to Peggy, 'after we'd broken up that winter, but kept in increasingly warm and frequent touch, that I could keep away from him no longer and said, look, the 11th is a Sunday this year, would it be playing with fire if we met again? And on April 11th last year we snatched a night on the Île de France, in an impossibly small hotel room with a garrulous plumbing system and noctambulists boisterous outside our window as we made love. He often said to me, whatever happens to us, wherever we are in the world, we will spend April 11th together, won't we? As long as we live? Even just a phone call? – And now this. We were caught in a complicated triangle, the three of us. That spring of 1980 was quite something: that I should meet the two most important people of my life within a week or two of each other is extraordinary. I feel that my love for you, Peggy, is forever bound up with this poor doomed youth, as you called him. He loved you deeply – you represented a principle of life to him, of hope, in fact – that most rare and precious commodity. If anyone will keep him alive now, it will be us.'

Not least because *Total Eclipse* had somehow, on so many levels, embodied our three-way relationship, I thought again and again of Verlaine's speech at the end of the play: 'I remember our first summer, how happy it was, the happiest time of my life. Wandering across Belgium, eating turnips and huddling in ditches. He's not dead, he's trapped inside of me. As long as I live, he has some kind of flickering and limited life. It's always the same words and the same gestures – the same images: I walk behind him across a steep ploughed field; I sit, talking to him in a darkening room, until I can barely see his profile and his expressive hand; I lie in bed at dawn and watch him sleeping and see how nervously his hand brushes at his cheek. I remember him of an evening and he lives.' David Hare had said then that I didn't understand about the dark; now I did.

Part Two

13

When I came back from Geneva, nothing was the same, nor has it ever been since. Peggy and I shared this terrible thing, almost as if Aziz had been our child. This was in the ominous year of 1984, which more than exceeded its awful promise for us. Death seemed everywhere around. The director Alan Schneider, whom I knew slightly and Peggy knew well – he it was to whom she had given *Godot* and introduced him to 'whoever it was that wrote it' – was killed by a motorbike at Swiss Cottage as he crossed the road on his way to rehearsal at the Hampstead Theatre. Then my brilliantly gifted friend Drew Griffith, co-founder of Gay Sweatshop, died in dark circumstances, in a state of mental distress, killed by a dangerous, violent man whom he seems to have picked up deliberately, knowing the danger. 'Another sacrificial offering to the savage god of our generation,' I wrote to Peggy. 'I was flicking through my address cards yesterday, and pulled out Drew's, to tear it up. The telephone number was written in pencil – in Aziz's hand. That little red box is becoming a card index of death. Who sapped these kids' inner resources? How, at the age of thirty, could they have completely exhausted their appetite for life? The first letter I picked up when I got back yesterday was from my ex-dresser at the Albery saying that this letter would not be easy to write, because he was lying in bed in a psychiatric hospital. Two days after starting work on *The Clandestine Marriage*, he'd plunged into suicidal depression, collapsed and been taken to the Middlesex, which is where he is now. He apologised for the letter not being very sparkling, and thought he'd better sign off while he was still at least lucid: the nurse was just about to give him his medication, which makes him quite gaga. What is going on? This lovely ebullient 21-year old, full of fun and rushing about in all directions at once, reduced to a turnip in a psychiatric ward. I've written to him telling him that I'll come and see him at any time, and that if he wants anything at all I'll get it for him; but above all I told him how immensely fond of him I am. No doubt, parentless, he feels exceptionally alone in the world. As we all do.'

Peggy herself started a punishing course in chemotherapy. 'Just returned from my Middlesex second,' she wrote. '(I have thirteen!) The treatment is killing – specially if you study the fellow patients! The hospital is *horrid* – lines of hopeless despairing people. The radiotherapy makes me giddy: now this week I have it three times – plus two investigations. Then two per week, then three per week (beginning of June). One is either killed or cured.' Throughout it, much against my advice, and everyone else's, she reported to the office every day for work. I wrote to her as she had so often written to me, counselling calm and rest. My advice to her had as little effect as hers to me. Eventually, she recovered completely, physically, at any rate, but something had gone out of her. Perhaps it would be more true to say that something had got into her: fear. For the first time in her life, she was aware of her frailty, and though her will had conquered the tumour, her self-confidence had taken a battering. 'I'm just a little scared,' she wrote – a word hitherto absent from her vocabulary –

'about the side-effects and what it is doing to my system.' She no longer celebrated herself as she had so infectiously done before, and the always delicate balance in her between optimism and pessimism decisively shifted in favour of the latter.

Things seemed to get worse and worse on every level. *On the Spot* had been even less successful in the West End than at Watford; people simply didn't want it. I had come back from Capri somewhat purged of grief, but in no mood to give myself over to the murderous posturings of Perelli, in a play without an ounce of generous feeling in it. I radically modified my performance, making it extrovert instead of inward-turned as at Watford, but nothing could make it enjoyable. Finally, thankfully, it closed after two wretched weeks. Glad though I was to be rid of it, there was still a terrible sense of failure attached to the premature closure. On the last Saturday the company and I had a sort of wake in my dressing room, from which two of my guests who had seen the show that night, a young friend and a friend of his, J., returned with me to my flat, where we drank even more, and where I was to my surprise passionately embraced by J., which was a bewildering and disturbing experience, from which I shakily detached myself and stumbled off to bed alone. The next day, the Sunday, the young men and I went for lunch, where we all became fairly drunk all over again and very emotional, partly on account of the fact (which seemed miraculous to us at the time) that J. and I shared a birthday, then I went on to an afternoon gala auction in favour of – what? I can't remember – where I successfully bid £150 for a signed copy of *Citizen Ken*, a study of the life and works of Ken Livingstone; collecting my proud trophy, I made a shameless public pass at the gala's Master of Ceremonies, drank yet more, and then was poured by good friends into a cab. Arriving at my flat, I crawled up the stairs, smashing as I went the glasses I had brought back from my dressing room the previous night. Somehow noting that it was five o'clock, and knowing that I had a date to take Peggy to the première of the film *Another Country* at 7, I decided to refresh myself with a nap for an hour. I awoke from this four hours later, threw water on my face, and ran at high speed to Peggy's place, which was in darkness. Appalled to think that she may have gone ahead on her own, I rang the bell again and again.

A light went on; bolts were drawn back, and there, in a nightmarish reprise of my encounter with her on the night of our *souper sur l'herbe* four years earlier, was Peggy, this time in her night-gown with a shawl over her shoulders, still bruised from the chemotherapy, and toothless: she had removed her dentures to sleep. She looked unimaginably old and tiny, the little old crone of a fairy tale. 'I've come to take you to the film. I'm late. Terribly late.' I was still breathless, barely coherent, and, I suddenly realised, still rather drunk. She seemed bewildered. Hadn't I got her message? She had felt too ill to go the première, so cried off. I apologised profusely, and made to go. 'You'd better come in,' she said, herself again, despite appearances. Walking down the hall, just as she had four years earlier, she lit up lamps, restored her teeth, made me coffee, talked, listened. We heard some music. She gave me more wine. I wept, partly for shame at having dragged her from her sickbed, but also for all the terrible events of this terrible year. We talked some more. Finally, I went, she bidding me good-bye very gravely, not in sorrow, much less in anger, but rather as if she had seen a part of me that she'd never seen before. She seemed muted in contemplation of what we had come to: her old and ill, me drunk and despairing.

The lost weekend came to an end. She got better; I sobered up; life went on. She became quite aggressive about her well-being: 'I'm absolutely OK – and have been having a splendid time: very spoiled. I'm more than OK and have been having a wonderful time.' She disapproved of the life I was leading more than ever. 'It's the rushing about from one sensation to the next which exhausts the spirit. Surely your energies can be put to better use?' She had come into my flat when I was away filming and had found it in a mess. 'I didn't understand how, two weeks after your play had closed, you didn't even have time to clear all your waste baskets and it seemed to symbolise the life you lead – mounds of carelessly collected *rubbish*. It's all such a *waste*, as you trivialise yourself and your world.' I meanwhile began a descent into complete emotional chaos. I had got in touch with J., of whom I had found myself thinking often since our first hectic meeting. I saw him on a number of subsequent occasions, finally ending up in bed with him. With terrifying speed, I fell in love with him with a desperate intensity, fuelled by everything that had happened in the last few months. Soon, I was in the grip of an *amour fou* like none I had ever known, quite different from the romantic and erotic ardour of my feelings for Aziz. This passion shook me like a rat. I pursued it with insane, self-destructive compulsion; J., a remarkable and, as it happens, predominantly heterosexual young man, behaved towards me with a finesse and a sensitivity astonishing in one so young – one, moreover, who was himself in a desperate condition, his back against every imaginable wall. With perfect calm, so different to my emotional intemperateness, he healed the immediate wound left by Aziz's death. 'The first night we spent together,' I wrote to Peggy, 'when I lay in his arms I started to cry, deep terrible sobs, why exactly even I don't know, and he held me tight in his broad young arms as if I was drowning and he was saving me, and just said: "It's OK, it's OK". And it was.' But the seeds of terrible self-destruction were contained in the relationship. I contrasted myself, at 35 clearly heading for – hurtling towards – an early mid-life crisis, with him, wiser, as I saw it, more experienced, more alive, above all braver than me. 'The worst of it has been how old it has made me feel. He's so free, so open, has given himself so much to life despite wretched family circumstances. By comparison I seem never to have lived; seem to have cut off so much, running from one thing to the next, from one picture of myself to the next and never finding the centre. All of which you know, and I know, inside out. I seem unable to break out of the circle, however, and this guy has brought it home to me most upsettingly.' We each knew the other to be on the brink, and found strength in extending support to the other. For a while we lived together, but even after he'd gone we remained passionately close despite his other affairs, and the many complications of the rest of his life. It was the purest of all my passions so far, but also the most hopeless.

Of course I saw that this was a reaction to Aziz's death, and to some extent to Aziz's life, or rather, to the life we had had together. I had an aching need to find another channel for the love that he had unlocked in me, to keep love alive in me. I felt, with what degree of self-deception I cannot say, that Aziz would have approved, that it was he who had taught me to love like this. But I also knew full well that this was no mere act of transference. It was J. himself that I loved. The qualities I had attributed to him were real. By bizarre chance, I had met him at the most inopportune moment possible; moreover, there could clearly be no future for us. There could barely be a present. But I was defenceless, in the wake of Aziz's death, to resist such an overpowering attraction. However unsatisfactory it might be, it must run its course. In exchange, I offered J. my unconditional love, in perpetuity, a thing he had never previously received from any quarter, and promised to help him make his life whatever it was that he wanted it to be.

Peggy disapproved of the relationship, violently and without qualification, and said so again and again. She didn't understand it, or didn't want to. 'I am absolutely *shocked* at what you are doing. You are going to turn that young man into a spiv, living on you. Do you pay for his food? His expensive taste in drink (vodka), his taxis, his laundry, his theatre tickets?' She was appalled at the effect that it would have on me and my professional commitments, the newly commissioned translation of Milan Kundera's play *Jacques and His Master*, for example. 'Are you going to get any hours of privacy for sustained work? What do I say to Fabers? Do you simply want to take a commission from McCrum and Faber and spend it on this folly?' The aspect of the whole business of which she disapproved most violently, curiously enough, was my strong desire to nurture J., to encourage him to channel the gifts which might so easily disappear in the rush of immediate and readily available gratification, sexual, narcotic, alcoholic. 'You will destroy this boy – he has to learn and go to college, equip himself for a life of *self* support.' But that was exactly what I was trying to lead him towards. More than anything in his life he cared for writing, and I did everything I could to encourage him in that. Of course I romanticised him, seeing him as my very own Rimbaud. This was not entirely far-fetched: he resembled him physically, with the same sort of sawn-off beauty, and had the same arrogant radicalism of extreme and brilliant youth; we were certainly going through a season in hell. As soon as I could, I introduced him to Peggy, a ridiculous notion: they stared at each other uncomprehendingly across the generations, each in spectacles, he in his long overcoat, with holes in his trousers and his shoes falling apart, looking like a refugee from Stalingrad, she gaily attired in a summery frock. Both fell almost completely silent as I clumsily tried to explain each to the other. 'Peggy is negotiating with the National Theatre at the moment...J. is writing a novel.' It was agonising, and never repeated. '*Writing* forsooth!' she thundered afterwards. 'He can do this in his spare time and prove he is some good. Yes, you are going to spoil him for life, and neglect your own career – INFIRM OF PURPOSE!!' She was equally contemptuous of my impulse to help him sort himself out. People, she said, should sort themselves out; that was how characters were built. It was clear to me that my need to cherish another human being was stronger even than my need to be cherished, and the same was and always had been true of Peggy. 'So many love affairs leave little but the memory of ecstasy but one *should* leave one's mark on everyone one loves – help *create* a human being. You are so aware of this that I don't know why I mention it,' she had once written to me.

Justifying my behaviour with J., I wrote to her, 'A life like mine, without responsibility for any other, is somewhat against the natural law, and when God throws someone up who needs looking after, and whom I find I love, then I do it. Quite obviously, as both he and I know, J. has to work out a sensible future, and that may, probably will, involve more education (more exams, at any rate), but I approve of his present resolve to learn his maturity from the world, from work, from finding a means of sustaining himself. I shall hover a bit in the wings, like a godfather; that's all. And after all, if I have these philanthropic tendencies, they come from one person and one alone: you. The way in which you cared for me has been my example and the only way I could ever pay it back would be to do the same for someone else.' She was not to be mollified by any of this. 'I am enclosing a cutting in today's Standard which says that a firm which advertised for a school-leaver received four answers and only one turned up. They were offering between £5,000 and £6,000 a year which is around £90 per week. I feel that anyone who is encouraging young people not to work, who prefer to live on £45 per week from the Social Security (which is taken away from every worker) and who battens onto people who *do* work, should realise that in a few years time England will be totally on its uppers. These young people who don't learn any language, craft, or career, and who have no character, will simply lie about and nobody will be able to afford to keep them and the Social Security will collapse, so that they won't get that either. I think it is so disgusting that there are tens of thousands of young people who have no idea that they are living off other people, and they think themselves so talented and bright and are so pleased with themselves, whereas they are simply slobs with no character and very little talent.'

Peggy violently rejected suggestions that she herself might be possessed of any maternal instinct, primary or secondary; she had never wanted, she insisted, to have children, and her whole purpose with her authors was to make them free, independent, especially of her. In fact, I suspect that she had almost monstrously over-developed maternal instincts, and that she could never have trusted herself with an actual child of hers not to overwhelm it with love and attention. In addition, she had herself detested being a child, and had no desire to inflict the state of childhood on another creature. This was a point of absolute contact between us. And yet we both longed to help another human being heal itself, realise its full potential; both found the spectacle of talent or beauty going to waste unbearable. Once, startlingly, she had said to me: 'Should we adopt a child, you and I?' I was for once completely unable to respond at all. 'Would that be a good idea? Would it?' she asked. I burst out laughing. 'God, Peggy, I – ' 'You don't think it would be a good idea?' 'I simply can't imagine it, Peggy.' 'I suppose not.' She wasn't laughing. 'We could send some money to a Vietnamese child,' I said, 'keep him or her alive.' 'Yes, we could.' And we did. The moment had passed, thank God.

She never allowed that my, admittedly complex, feelings for J. were of this order. She saw it as vanity and indulgence. 'Try *properly* to adjust that boy's life – he MUST LIVE ALONE and he MUST WORK, or he will be destroyed. Don't help spoil his life.' Of course she was right that the whole thing was fraught with pitfalls; but between us, J. and I got him on the road to recovery, despite Peggy's dark forebodings. I believe there was another factor, too, in her attitude to my relationship with J.: the intense three-way relationship, ending so blackly, between Peggy, Aziz and me, had been a cauterising experience for her which she was not going to repeat. She saw the increasing intensity of my feelings for J., which brought me to the brink of despair, almost with a touch of Schadenfreude: 'In spite of all you have felt, and are feeling, you don't understand when I lash out at you. It's because I care so much and I feel a need to destroy what I feel and be done with it. If only we didn't feel so much and if only we could accept. I think this feeling for J. must surely have given you an insight? For the first time you have seen you can't have it all. *I* find this difficult and therefore I seek to destroy my feelings, so that I can have NOTHING.' When, at the very beginning of my relationship with J., he had gone to Spain on holiday with friends and, desperately unhappy, had run away, I immediately flew there to reclaim him, not just from Spain but from the drugged oblivion that I knew he was looking for. I hadn't even got a reliable address, but eventually I found him and brought him back. There were in him equal impulses towards life and its opposite; the example of Aziz made me determined to pull him away, by force if necessary, from any incipient romance with death, and in this I succeeded. Peggy was unimpressed, uninvolved. What she liked was when I fell hopelessly in love with someone from afar and endured character-building torment. J., meanwhile, came and went. He turned his hands to various jobs, fell in with disparate crowds of friends, experimented with all sorts of substances, and wrote feverishly; from time to time he and I connected with fierce tenderness. The flat was at the very least a place to which he could return at any time, and I extended to him, as I had promised, support and unquestioning, unconditional love, of both of which he availed himself.

My friendship with Peggy continued more fretfully than it had. We could never recapture, naturally, the intoxicating quality of the first few months of our friendship, though even they had been clouded with anguish, on her part. There was affection, but not so much fun, not the same sense of mutual delight. Often, there was a sense of terrible frustration, which I now see was largely occasioned by Peggy's sense that she had surrendered to me the thing that she prized above all else: her independence. Somehow I had become a part of her which she could not ignore. There was an extraordinary eruption one night at the end of the unrelentingly dreadful 1984 when we went to Covent Garden to see the first night of John Schlesinger's new production of *Der Rosenkavalier. Rosenkavalier* was a central work in her life. Strauss was her composer, representing in sound the land of heart's desire for her, voluptuous, tender and potentially savage, a sexual world full of ache and enchantment, and this particular work became central to our friendship, though we never actually spelt out the parallels, never acknowledged the resonances for us contained in the story of the older woman who acknowledges that she must lose the younger man. If I was an unlikely Oktavian, she was the Marschallin to the life. My first glimpse of her at Covent Garden that evening was arresting, so much so that I actually stood for a minute or two looking at her across the foyer before I greeted her. She was wearing a new fur coat with its collar up around her ears, giving her the air of one of the Straussian sopranos of her youth, Lotte Lehmann or Elisabeth Schumann, exuding a glamorous intensity which made her stand out immediately in a crowd whose whole purpose in life was competitive glamour. Despite this, she seemed nervous, and had a troublingly persistent cough. After our usual peck of greeting, she said, gravely, 'We're all in deep mourning.' A play which she represented and which I had deeply wanted to do, and seemed to be about to able to do, had slipped away from me. This was my first intimation of it.

It was a blow, definitely. I was winded for a moment. The play had been written with me in mind; it was a superb piece of work and I had been shattered to find that someone else was being offered it. When it seemed that that someone else was not going to do it after all, and when it was then tantamount to being offered to me again, I had allowed myself, fatally and foolishly, to think that it was in the bag. Peggy must have known the moment the decision was made, and she had been unable to resist telling me what had happened. Now, seeing the black cloud on my face, she bitterly regretted doing so, because it threatened to spoil our evening. I made light of it, tried to forget about it, but she was irresistibly drawn to discussing it through the first interval. By the end of the Second Act, however, the silvery perfection of Barbara Bonney's effortless ascent into soprano heaven during the Presentation of the Rose had worked its usual magic, and in its after-glow we finally banished the tedious realities of careers and their hopes and disappointments. At the end of the evening, with the final great trio of renunciation, resignation and reconciliation still hanging in the air, we went off gaily to have supper at Bertorelli's, and talked of this and that, the music, the food, the Opera House: anything but *that* play. Peggy was coughing worse and worse and it seemed to me that I needed to get her home as soon as possible, which I did, settling the bill and getting us into a taxi as soon as possible. I duly sent her a card saying how wonderful it had been to see her 'however depleted by December's depredations we both might have been' and signed off by urging her to take vitamins. The next day, I returned home to find a beautiful bow-tie and an exquisite clothes brush waiting for me in my front room. A day after that, there was a card from her, replying to mine: 'Got your card. *I* thought it was a really HORRIBLE evening – your Brummel persona went on and *on* about the hairs on your coat, and at dinner you snapped "Oh, stop coughing!" I realise you were preoccupied because of the news I spilled inadvertently, but I hope you were satisfied at being chauffeured back home as soon as you wanted.'

Would this year's miseries never end? Days later, I wrote a letter to her: 'Only now do I feel able to answer your card. It hurt me bitterly. You were tired. I was tired. You were ill. All night I thought of nothing but your tiredness and how risky it was for you to be there at all. I hastened through supper as quickly as possible. In the taxi afterwards I refrained from coming with you to Redcliffe Square because I knew you would invite me in, and that that would keep you up even later. During the course of the evening I made a few no doubt very feeble jokes, a couple of them in the form of teases about your moulting coat, and once I joked about your coughing. After five minutes I had dismissed the information about the play as merely the latest, hopefully perhaps the last, disappointment of 1984. Your card was unkind and unfair, and it is not the first time you have been either of those things to me. Do you know your own strength? When you attack, you wound deeply. Do I really disappoint and disgust you so much? That's certainly how it feels. I am as low in reserves as can be: low, low, low, in the bloody gutter. Meanwhile, I also have to thank you for the incredibly beautiful case and the bow-tie. The satirical significance of the clothes brush only became apparent after your card arrived. Your Christmas presents have been sitting here since Friday night. I would like to deliver them to you. Do you want to see me?'

I didn't send the letter at once. It was all I could do to write it. I was crumbling on all fronts. Things were very bad between me and J., who was still living with me, but unhappily; I felt that he despised and resented me. That being so, I could see no point in anything whatever. I became almost paralysed, mechanically performing my daily duties. One evening I sat at home immobile in the dark, unable to move, my body turned to lead, feeling my brain with frightening realism to be some kind of hinge out of which the pin was slowly being pulled; when the pin came out, my mind would fall apart. This was seven o'clock. I was doing a one-man play at the Bush Theatre at the time; at eight I had a performance. For the first time ever in my professional life, I contemplated missing a show, simply not showing up. Somehow, as if sleep-walking, I got myself to the theatre, arriving five minutes before the show was due to start, and played it in a sort of trance. In the middle of the show, I broke down and talked gibberish for a minute or two, absolute gibberish, loony-talk. Then I continued, as if nothing had happened. I contacted no-one, went to two Christmas parties in the desperate hope of throwing all this off, but fled one and got monstrously, incoherently drunk at the other. I trudged like a zombie round Harrods, Selfridges, wherever, looking for presents for people who didn't need or want anything, knowing that they would be doing exactly thing the same for me. The whole thing seemed surreal and hateful.

It was then that Peggy's card arrived. After writing the first letter, I wrote another, a day later, explaining it, and sent both. The covering letter ended: 'I don't intend to go on. I only mention it to explain why your presents, the only ones that gave me any pleasure to buy, bought long before the others, never came to you, and why I never thanked you for the beautiful bag, the brush and the bow-tie. I figured that they had been sent after *Rosenkavalier*, and therefore to the person whose deeply unattractive behaviour you described on the card. All in all it was the *coup de grâce* of 1984, this filthy year, a parting kick in the teeth, the last failure to add to the unending list. I've failed pretty well everyone this year, producers, fellow-writers, lovers. And now you. That, at any rate, was how I felt when I got the card. Fortunately, the black blanket of smog has risen. J. and I have amicably resolved what was wrong: he has a place of his own and is leaving at the earliest possible opportunity. The laughably-entitled Festive Season has gone away. In the hope that you might be working, I came to your office on the Friday after Christmas, like Uncle Vanya with my little parcel in my hand; but you weren't there. I've written six letters to you, all of which I've torn up. I phoned you both in London and Brighton yesterday to speak to you at the start of a NEW YEAR. No luck. Well, I do wish you a most happy new year, a most happier new year. I would like very much to see you and give you these things that I believe you would like. I want to dissolve the – is it a misunderstanding? – that has come between us. I want to see you. Full stop.'

14

Somehow, again, we resolved all that, and 1985 immediately showed a considerable improvement over its predecessor. But between Peggy and me, something was still slightly sour. Apart from anything else, she felt that she was sharing me with too many people. On one occasion I had suggested that we go together to the unveiling of a plaque to Allen Lane. 'No, I don't of course want to go to the Penguin do – but for Tony Godwin Penguin would have disappeared, as he rescued it, with the most wonderful new titles and format. So successful was it that Allen Lane threw him out (and that isn't my partisan opinion). He was absolutely filled with hatred and jealousy. Nor do I want to meet you afterwards. You will have been talking your head off to dozens of other people and you won't remember what you have told me and what you have told them. I have discovered this in the past. It's a kind of continuous "performance", almost a "record" and you have exhausted yourself and your mind is muddled and wound up and I'm just someone else to go on talking to. One has the feeling that you have a long list of people you feel you have to – or even want to – meet, but you are so busy rushing from one to another, ticking off the list, fitting them all in – so conscientiously – that you don't really know *exactly* who you are with at the time itself. I'm not *complaining* – I'm just avoiding you when you are rushing from all the things you *have* to do, and all the people you *have* to see!' My answer was somehow not an answer at all: 'What you say about my social calendar is of course true but NOT what you say about the state in which I come to you: I have NEVER, not ONCE, spoken to you as if you were someone else: you are not a person one confuses with another, my god PLEASE do let's meet soon', and my p.s. was equally unavailing: 'I daren't say how much I'd love to see you because you'll accuse me of FITTING YOU IN, so instead I'll say how much I'd love you to FIT ME IN somewhere soon.'

Essentially, I agreed with her diagnosis of the malaise of my life. Until very recently, it had seemed wonderful, a merry-go-round of unflagging delight, but events in my emotional life plus a kind of professional exhaustion had now conspired to rob it of a lot of its charm. At one of my not infrequent financial crises, Peggy had sent me a cheque, and I had written a thank you letter returning it to her which expressed some of this: 'It won't do, will it? It's nonsense, and humiliating nonsense at that, to be unable to pay perfectly ordinary, regular bills when they crop up. It's a symptom of a deep fatuousness at the heart of my life. I suppose books, records and meals account for the worst of my over-spending. And while it's true that I always listen to the records with at least an ear and a half; and I always read some of the books, and they will all come in useful eventually; and one does have to eat – the fact is that I could find ample nourishment in a tenth of the books and records and could just as well cook at home. The woeful fact is that all this spending is really CONSOLATION. It's a sort of self-stroking to assuage just what nameless grief I couldn't begin to tell you. The moment I'm left alone with myself, away from people but above all denied action of some kind, an emotional pea-souper spreads through me, permeating every inch of my being. If I buy something it seems to dispel it, less, I think, because I've acquired something, than because it implies the future: when I get home I'll read this, I'll listen to that. I find the idea of a future peculiarly intangible, most of the time; and when, as now, my future is so choppy and fragmented, I quickly lapse into a state of catatonia. Oddly for someone as fleshly as I am, I live always with the feeling that I might drift away altogether, like a little boat that's slipped its moorings, away onto the ocean, bobbing meaninglessly about. It's all nonsense, utter, utter nonsense, the books, the records and the meals. At least I'm not buying heroin; but what I am buying is scarcely less of an evasion, an escape.'

Her reply came by return of post. 'What you write about yourself,' she wrote, 'is horribly horribly true. Your constant need for stimulation – friends, shopping, filling every single moment to stop yourself being alone, is exactly as if you need heroin. Life isn't continuously charged with excitement and incident – you have got to learn to be alone and to do nothing. You need Krishnamurti's *Fear of the Known*. It's my only copy and the only Krishna book worth reading *Word for Word*. It's in the office and I will collect it for you. I understand EXACTLY what's the matter – I share some of this mania. I love shopping for instance – can't really control this, and I like to fill my time too with reading, listening etc. But I've cut out PEOPLE which is an enormous help as I don't find most of them interesting. Yes, the first time one meets someone, something is yielded – but I would rather come home to my friends (Gide, Mann and any really good book). Of course you are happy acting because you get your adrenaline and you cannot live without it. Yet it's NOT the way to live. There should be waves and troughs – a rhythm.' Then she started to get seriously alarmist. 'Your illness is MUCH more difficult to cure than drink or drugs because it's what you think life SHOULD BE – whereas it's not even good for your acting because you pour too much into it. You intoxicate yourself with any part and the character part is only intoxicated at certain peaks – to write your character on the stage would exhaust an audience. I don't think a doctor of any kind can help. You MUST accept the shallows of life and then rejoice at the peaks. You will have to take a few sessions of complete relaxation – steady breathing, letting the mind wander. (Krishnamurti's demand.) Well NOW YOU KNOW. Can you SAVE yourself?'

This apocalyptic feeling about me extended to the world at large. Though so many of her writers were strongly left-wing, Peggy was not herself allied to any particular political philosophy, but as the industrial confrontations which brought Margaret Thatcher to power became more and more militant, she became increasingly dismayed by the state of the nation. 'What are we all UP to? We seem to take on things which now take *us* on – you and Hare frantically directing two very difficult, almost impossible plays (diffi-cult and impossible for different reasons, of course) – both *self-inflicted.*' I was directing *The Infernal Machine;* Hare, *King Lear.* 'Here we are with England collapsing morally and financially and we are frantically running about like chickens without heads. That BLOODY Thatcher – now she is trying to blow up an Arab *explosion.* She *must* have her wars, whereas the country is *definitely* going *seriously* broke, thousands are homeless, everyone is kidding themselves that we are all OK – and now,' she continued, in a surreal flight of unreason, 'the *computers* are showing their ugly teeth and trying to destroy the Big Bang!! It's laughable; it's absurd. What is DRIVING us to this frantic whirl of useless endeavour? It's a kind of despair, and fear of stopping and asking ourselves questions!' She began to be obsessed by this theme. 'We don't discuss what is, in my case, a matter that is filling my thoughts, and particularly when I get up each morning. What should we all do? We just pretend it's not there, but society is breaking down and being actively pushed by the powerful, ruthless unions and the people behind them. The railway crisis can't be solved without a breaking down of the railways, and that will lead to all militant workers refusing to see "reason". That it's self-destructive doesn't matter to them – it's part of their passion and hatred (and self-hatred). I'm finding it dreadfully difficult to continue at the office, as many of our authors are breaking down and panicking, yet no plays are being written to cover any of this. The cause now is a mental one: it is not just economic – we have brought our economic disaster on ourselves.'

She became strongly opposed to the socialist position. 'Regards the present "crisis", the state of play at the moment has nothing whatever to do with the country under Heath. The change is in Labour itself. They repudiate the Far Left, they don't want chaos. The TUC represent Tories just as much as Labourites. Affluence has made the Left love comfort and money and foreign travel and the freedom to spend money AS THEY WISH. Therefore they want to support some of the Tory world until such time as they know what they can do and what needs to be done. Thatcher is a ruthless theoretical woman and she doesn't care what damage is being done so that she can get the country on its feet. She destroys her own "class" as much as Labour. When a small business collapses, she says "Never mind, another will take its place". She's like an army general: it doesn't matter how many troops die in battle as long as the battle is won. In this present crisis, Kinnock, if you please, is SILENT, and he leaves it to Hattersley (who has come out of this very well) to say that the NGA *should* keep the law. Kinnock is simply a doll the Labour people want to use as a front. Don't forget, the affluent society is as much a Labour society as a Tory. Keep an eye on Heffer. I wish he were to become PM at some future date. Unfortunately he is chairman of the party, not the head, and there are a bad group of Labour people in the cabinet, just as there are an effectively ludicrous group of Tories with the Female Fury at their head, dreaming of some kind of UK which is admirable but poor. The way of getting it is like Verdun!'

At some point I had reported to her that my friend Snoo Wilson and I had had a falling out over Margaret Thatcher, I regarding her as merely embodying the revenge of the *petite bourgeoisie*, he, like many of my generation, seeing her as the devil incarnate, posing a more fundamentally damaging threat to the essential fabric of British life than Hitler ever had. Thereafter Peggy cast Snoo in her mind in the unlikely role of principal prophet of the disintegration of society. 'I can imagine that Snoo is shouting with pleasure at England's failure to land the six billion Plessey contract. On the air today a socialist was saying how delighted he was to have Mrs T "humiliated" and the interviewer said, "I suppose you don't even *think* of the loss to the British economy, as long as you can score a point against Mrs T" !!! (The socialist was floored.) Another problem about the Left is the fact that they passionately want to bring EVERYONE

DOWN, and make a grey equal. Yet the average working-class man wants to climb up and become middle-class! You have only to see the TUC on television to see that they are NOT cloth-caps any longer, but really nice suits, white shirts and ties. They want televisions, three-piece suites, nice holidays etc; they *don't* want to live in terraces with a week's hol in Blackpool – they now drink *wine* etc. It's this envy, hatred and malice and passion for lies I find so absolutely *disgusting*. What has Snoo tried to do for his country? What sort of example is he of the Ideal Englishman? Why sneer and destroy unless you try to do something yourself?'

She was not the only person thinking these thoughts in Britain in the mid-eighties, of course, but there was a kind of rage, a sort of fear, behind her expression of them, which was new. In fact, after 1984, everything was different: she was, I was, life was. A year after J. and I had met – and therefore a year after Aziz's death – he had embarked on an intense relationship with a woman almost as old as I was, although we remained intensely close, and I had met B., and we had become lovers. It was a very different sort of affair from the others, much calmer, more grown-up, not in the least predicated on *amour fou*. 'B. reveals more and more depth and stability,' I wrote to her, 'and I find myself feeling more and more for him. I'm desperately trying to check my passion – it's a useless emotion, and so unattractive. If I give in, I'll lose him. He quite rightly prefers to proceed step by step; I long not merely to run before I can walk, but to fly. Whenever I try to talk about *us*, him and me, the way I have always done with any lover, he cuts it short very gently: "Don't," he simply says. I don't understand this man, but I am learning something quite unexpected from him.' In theory, she should have approved of the relationship, but it meant nothing to her – or perhaps she saw it as such a different thing from the sort of passion about which she and I had talked with such mutual understanding in the past that she felt there was now no common chord between us on these matters. B. and I went away to Switzerland for a while, where he cooked and we talked and he showed me the world. 'As we stroll around he gently instructs me in those matters of which I am so deeply ignorant; the names of the trees and the birds, the behaviour of the plants and the soil, the habits of the weather.' Exactly what she had been prescribing for me since we had first met, and yet Peggy never engaged with this relationship at all, and when, four years later, it came to an end, and I met someone else, Peggy rather off-handedly said to B., of the new relationship, 'How long will it last?' to which B. had had no answer. 'Well,' said Peggy, 'he'll certainly be able to give him plenty of side-shows.' She seemed to have lost faith in my capacity for passion.

By this time, my acting career was well-established in the theatre, television and film; I started to direct; and thanks entirely to her efforts, I had become a writer. Our closest professional experience had been over *Being an Actor*. Peggy was less directly involved with my subsequent books; in the end, after all, she was a play agent, and I was not a playwright (as she pointed out rather forcefully on the two occasions in our time together when I attempted dramatic form: a play about Edward Gordon Craig's Moscow *Hamlet* – abandoned – and *Nicolson Fights Croydon*, at the Offstage Theatre. 'You are NOT a playwright yet and perhaps never will be and these awful monologues!') She was however very interested in my work as a director. She would have made an excellent director herself. I suspect that at a critical moment in her life, when she was running Q Theatre, she could have become a director rather than a literary agent, but some voice deep inside told her that it was presumptuous of her. She had without qualification adored management. 'Running a theatre is bliss,' she once wrote to me. 'Very responsible, and no passing the buck. You must do it in a few years' time.'

My first attempt at directing was *Loving Reno* by Snoo Wilson, which the author and I co-directed, in theory, but in fact, rapidly acquiring a taste for the job, I somewhat hijacked the production, and was quickly writing to Peggy about as if I were Max Reinhardt, or at the very least Frith Banbury: a seasoned pro. 'I don't think I've done anything as tiring as directing. You have to be 100% present at every minute, thinking of the play, the actors and the production simultaneously. You have to have an opinion about everything. You have to make the actors, the designer, the stage management and the theatre staff feel wonderful; but no one does this for you. You have to develop strength of character, and resist paranoia (they don't like me, they think I'm no good etc). At six o'clock you simply want to fall into bed: certainly not speak to anyone, but then you have to be at your most alert.' She came to see the show, and liked what she saw. 'I greatly admired the total professionalism of your production and the orchestration (above all) of the text and actors. I wasn't at all bored throughout, though the quirky subject doesn't greatly appeal. I'm not crazy about the leading man as an actor – he shouted too much and then switched into a pianissimo of an unsupported voice: it's a theatre, even if it is in the round, in the square, not a private space. (I have a phobia about unsupported voices when it's a matter of singing and this also applies for a straight play – there must be supported voices with a projection of even one yard.) I really liked the fat lady best, she was truly exotic and made me think of those two South American novels we have read recently. She seemed somehow authentic: if only everyone else had transported me into that exotic world.'

She took a passionate interest in my acting (though she would never come to a first night, and never let me know that she was in the house, preferring to slip in, as she put it, *en yashmak*, veiled and swathed in all-enveloping garments). She had more faith in my acting than anyone has ever had, including me; her feelings for me were closely bound up with her response to my work. 'You provide something so special as an actor – passion, poetry, presence, laughter, tears. Why do you think I wrote to *you* in the first place? I've never written to ANY other actor, or felt from them what you give as an artist. NOT A WORD of what I say about you is exaggerated, and you will SEE, you will *see*. My *only* talent is to *recognise* and usually before everyone sees things through my eyes – I'm usually two years or so ahead. So just don't think about it; just BE and everything I tell you will happen.' She was a very good judge of acting, and her advice, whether on character or on technical matters, was unerring. She had strong views about the voice, whether singing or speaking. 'Some time later on I want to ask you about your high register (when I was very young I studied singing with Frau Schadow, the teacher of Lotte Lehmann and Elisabeth Schumann, so I'm specially interested). The National Theatre is poor on *breath* in the upper registers – a certain blond – who shall be nameless – for instance, screams like a pea-hen when he becomes angry (on stage) all because he shuts off his breath. This old German woman made her pupils pull/draw up their breath *from the ground,* *through* the feet, and up to the head. This is how all those Wagnerian ladies were able to sing Brünnhilde – *everything relaxed* (à la Stanislavski!). It was a kind of *vomiting* (the way you vomit your middle register and lower register in Shakespeare). One had to boom a lieder lyric *in one breath* from beginning to end – not sing it – *vomit* it. The result in Elizabeth Schumann was quite something. Any effort or "attack" was done from *just above* the prick/cunt which was struck like a gong.'

Once I asked her about one of her roles as an actress. 'How strange it was for me to talk to you about Lady Macbeth! All I can recollect is a concentration of WILL – a purity of motive – never permitting the voice as an instrument but as a means of being the inexorable will behind Macbeth, as if every moment had to be concentrated on bringing him, driving him to power. The horrible feeling of contempt for him, yet a total obsession for this one thing – naked ambition for someone else (if only one could *become him!*). I understood Nixon, believe me!' Above all, she perceived acting as an art, and spoke so eloquently of it as such, that she shamed me out of developing weary habits. I shared her belief that every performance should be a kind of miracle, and strove however clumsily towards that ideal. She lavished her highest praise on me when she came to re-visit *The Beastly Beatitudes of Balthasar B* some months into the run: 'Dearest little chap – I've been subjecting myself to a dose of the West End, and it's left me with such a feeling of sympathy for the very few good and noble actors – it's a métier best suited to the superficially talented, but it must be HELL for the dedicated. I ended up last night in B.B. You were sweet and funny – like a mountain goat – lighter and more beguiling than before. I just don't know HOW you give an excellent dedicated performance to a somewhat ordinary play night after night after night, and the West End system is pretty hellish for actors. I wrote you a card (now torn up) crying off Thursday as far as I was concerned – but having seen you play last night I feel you all needed all the support you can get and I think I'd better feed you all at my home.' On the other hand, she would not abide self-indulgence, which she called 'whining,' her favourite term of abuse. On one occasion she fiercely admonished me: 'You can't have it ALL, at once! You can't expect the critics to give ALL to you, freely; roses all the way – at once – (or there's nothing left, you will have worn it all out). You ARE thrusting, making and taking every opportunity; very self-absorbed. These critics have been around for ages and they are sad, human, fearful, and they see you glorying in part after part, pushing your way to the top.' Then she made a characteristic segue: 'If McEnroe can face attack after attack (*much* worse than any you have had) then you must too. Everyone with outstanding talent is a source of envy to others. FOR GOD'S SAKE think about others, less fortunate, and be a GOOD, WISE, PUPPY.'

McEnroe was something of an obsession of hers: she followed his matches with awe and anguish, as well as considerable expertise; tennis had been her game. 'Pup,' she wrote to me after we'd been to the Festival Hall to hear *La Mer* and two other repertory war-horses, 'the concert was a most lovely idea: and to re-hear those three familiar works a very special pleasure – very soothing as I've been very strung up about McEnroe, who is an artist, not just a tennis player. Hope you saw him: so *brave*, so committed, so *marvellous* at his craft (or I should say *art*), so gutsy and unsentimental. Do look at his work. As you know, I feel you have much in common. He, too, has puppy qualities. There is this ferocious, *masculine* concentration of purpose in both of you: his match-playing is like your Mozart: almost *ugly* in its passion; but of course supremely beautiful. *Your* beauty is everything *you are*, and it's *strength* poured into a purpose. There is no need to "analyse" what you are doing, as if it's some kind of hobby or gift, or ask *why* you are doing it or what meaning life has. Life should and does *drive* you, and you should and do pour yourself into it.' She gloried in his bad behaviour: 'Little McEnroe was caught, too, in utter unreality – that rain kept on, with snatched patches of sunshine, and as Mark Cox said, *if only he'd been allowed to explode once*. But the strain of keeping himself in check was too much. In the third set (he'd won two) he was two points from winning the Championship, but the umpire heard him mutter "bald-headed eagle" – picked up by the mike! – and began his "Mr McEnroe – I must warn you . . . " etc etc and that great over-developed, over-gymmed, over-muscled unimaginative hulk Connors took full advantage. I know you respect discipline and will, but the incomparable beauty of McEnroe's playing, the exquisite co-ordination of arm, foot, body (so that he seems to be dancing on air) is heart-breaking. All the "experts" say he is the greatest player in the world today – but, like Nijinsky, he has a breaking point. He left London alone, sombre and silent, on the Concorde, on Sunday, obviously not knowing quite where he was, or what was happening. DON'T LAUGH – DON'T CONDEMN. Try and understand!'

I took her feelings very seriously. Of all the presents I ever gave her the one which meant most to her, which filled her with untrammelled delight, was a life-size cardboard-backed photograph of McEnroe which I had persuaded a highly suspicious sports shop in Wimbledon to let me have. It stood in her office for many months, to the mystification of the many world-famous authors, international producers and directors who passed through. On one occasion, she sent me a postcard on which she had written: '*Tennis through the Ages*: McEnroe merely *insults* the referee when he is palpably wrong, whereas I note Caravaggio quarrelled with his opponent *and stabbed him* during a game of tennis!' Every step in his career was held up as an example, dreadful or otherwise: 're little McE: it's better to fail than *not*, and be an artist. It's not winning or losing, it's the *development* of one's talents, and he's only 23. On Saturday he was playing a bit cautiously and seriously (his eyes were like little *snakes* as he waited for the opponent's service!) He's not quite so thin, and the extra few pounds were necessary (Oh not *fat*, but not quite so frail as last year!!) so don't get frail yourself – it's a BAD idea!' Inevitably, the ultimate betrayal of art in Peggy's book, he became involved with a woman. 'I had to switch off the McEnroe match – he was *doomed* – alas he gave up his art for life and the total intrusion of the little O'Neal girl (Tatum) has somehow got into his sinews. She and her father are, basically, *rubbish* and their life style cheap and hectic. It was *awful* to look at him (she and her dad were, of course, inevitably sitting conspicuously looking on).'

McEnroe was not the only sportsman whom she adored but in whom she eventually lost faith: 'Poor little Hurricane Higgins is losing his supremacy at snooker – he is drinking beer between every shot!!! I've had to switch off and come and write to you instead.' The standard she set for acting was as bracing and as demanding as the standard she set for writing and for tennis; it was in fact the same one: *absolute commitment*, in every word, every gesture, every stroke. She thought a real talent – for writing, singing, acting, sport – was a phenomenon as terrible as it was rare, and had to be served unstintingly. I suspect that she had long ago decided that she had no such talent, and this had made her the more insistent that those who did have it must not abuse it or fail it. In fact, I believe she may well have had considerable talent as either actress, director or writer (about her singing we can know nothing) but that in a curious act of denial not unlike her refusal of the idea of motherhood, she refused to commit herself to it, perhaps because she knew what it would have cost her, how the emotion would have swept through her like a desert wind. She was fierce in her criticism of my performances, but the criticism came from a position of extraordinary faith in my talent, which she felt, not without justice, that I constantly betrayed in favour of indulgences, whether social, emotional or professional. She was perfectly happy for me to write and direct, as – in her dismissive phrase – 'gifts or hobbies' – but more than anything she would have liked to have seen me fulfil the exceptional potential she believed me to possess as an actor. Alas, she never did.

Sometimes she was thrown from true judgement by her feelings about me; when I appeared in *The Kiss of the Spider Woman*, as Molina, the screaming queen who shares a prison cell with a revolutionary freedom fighter with whom he ultimately has a passionate affair, Peggy wrote to me that it was very fine, technically, of course, but surely I was miscast? I was far too masculine, she said, for such a part, for which many other actors were naturally right. I think the sight of me as effeminate and sexually passive was upsetting to her, the more so, perhaps, because I was generally held to be very convincing. Jealousy was another enormously strong element in Peggy's character; she could be jealous of almost anyone or anything. When I was playing Faust on the radio and discovering Goethe in all his astonishing variety, I wrote her a long impassioned letter about him and his work, assuming that she would share my enthusiasm. Instead she replied tartly that I must try to be less promiscuous in my passions. When I told her that I would be playing Napoleon in *The Man of Destiny* opposite the fascinating French actress Delphine Seyrig, she said, quite erroneously, 'A notorious Lesbian, you know.'

She crucified herself with jealousy over my friendship with Rupert Everett when we were appearing at the same time, but in different plays, in the West End, I in *The Beastly Beatitudes of Balthasar B*, he in *Another Country*. She went to see him in his show after I had mentioned him to her for the first time and wrote: 'Your new Best Friend' – the capitals were ominous – 'has a personality and performance of *great delicacy*.' I replied that I was delighted that she had liked Ru, as I called him, and rashly added, 'as in Du bist die Ru, I suppose,' a harmless little Schubertian joke which back-fired horribly. A suggestion that the three of us would meet was rejected: 'I just felt I couldn't face an evening with you and Rupe "in thrall," and me odd man out (Ziz all over again). So I decided to write you a card and to go to Liverpool instead. Then I saw your show and my heart *bled* for your bravery and I felt I should make an effort. If you ARE besotted, I'd rather not come on Wed (or Thurs) and can meet your friend on some more formal, shorter occasion. But if you *are* your own man, yes Wed will be fine.' I telephoned her immediately, but she was distant and the

164

conversation brief. I then sent her a new book I thought she'd be interested in with a card assuring her that I was indeed 'my own man'. She wrote back: 'so you understood my loss of equilibrium! When Martin hinted just before Paris that you'd entered into a new and very special friendship I had to begin to downgrade my position with you and accept being put into a further periphery of your life. At lunch you never mentioned R.E. except very casually (though I noticed you asked me if I'd liked him in the play) so I possibly enlarged the whole thing, and at that stage I felt I couldn't face that evening. But I've behaved BADLY, as you are a totally free man, and you've always told me yourself what there was to tell. I wasn't asleep when you phoned – I was slumped in total misery and simply couldn't respond. But your cards and the book broke down the wall between us.' Her postscript said: 'One always behaves badly if one loves. One also behaves badly if one is loved!!! You can't win.' And she sent me a book and some soup. I replied (accompanying a box of Brahms quartets): 'I totally utterly absolutely understand.' But we weren't out of the woods yet. 'Thank you for the Brahms – LOVELY. And the card in which what was NOT said spoke the truth louder than what WAS said. There is a whole world shared between actors with similar tastes, background and talents which sets them apart and together and which is very sweet and private. I think I should try and suspend communications and meetings and begin to let my thoughts flow *elsewhere*, in different directions, and stop the habit of thinking, when I see, read or hear something marvellous, "*I must tell Simon.*" – This letter is too full of *truths not said.*'

'As you wish, my darling Peggy, as you wish,' I wrote back. 'I do realise that I cause you unimaginable pain. I know that our relationship, and I suppose my character, who I am and the way that I behave in the world, not just to you, contains the most terrible frustrations. It's not really the point to say that if I didn't see you anymore, a huge gap would open up in my life which no one could ever fill, because *no one* has a tenth of your passion, your beauty, your sense of what's important in life, what matters and what doesn't. You've opened my eyes, my ears and my heart to so much, and our mutual enjoyment has been among the most exalted experiences of my life. But that's all selfish. I suppose it is wise not to spell things out; let what's unsaid but understood speak for us. *If* it is pain, torment, misery, then of course we must stop.' 'I too don't know what's best,' she wrote back. 'Certainly today I've been so unhappy to think that we were saying goodbye, that it was surface CALM and quiet because I was so *deeply* unhappy, and there was no one in the world to whom I could speak about it. I think the most shattering thing was that *you didn't tell me* and I learned it quite recently – for the first time, through Martin. The fact that you *aren't* lovers makes it almost worse for me, because I realise that you will be sharing with *him* all the most important feelings you have about music, art and so on. Ziz wasn't able to give you what I'm sure your Ru can and is giving you, and that the two of you are really complete in yourselves. I think if you'd told me earlier that you were growing into a deepening relationship, I might have been able to accept it – but I feel as if our last meetings and so on (specially that last lunch at Bussola, when I felt so uneasy) are *retrospectively* coloured by my now realising that you were totally committed to someone else and that I was just one of your many friends you enjoyed meeting. I feel absolutely shattered and humiliated to think that for weeks you have been thinking *totally* about someone else, while I was still behaving as if I were very special, and sending you letters etc. I *did* begin to notice that the letters were drying up and the postcards were superseding them!!! But I didn't realise that you'd given your *heart and mind* to someone. A true passionate friendship on both sides.'

'P.S,' she continued, 'Perhaps you should confirm this. If it is the case – unless he means so much to you that you don't want to mention it to anyone, as it's *holy*! Certainly Ziz was so very deficient in so many artistic ways, that it must be marvellous to be able to share all these things with one of *your own kind*. I don't want to be an occasional friend, and if you are now writing *him* the letters you used to write me, and reacting to all the marvels immediately to him, I think I am superfluous. As for my Birthday. Off to Liverpool Wed lunchtime and return Thursday lunch time (or early pm) so there's not much manoeuvrability – but if what I suspect is true (and I'm not usually wrong) and that you are his and he is yours, then I feel I should become a much more shadowy person in your life, and perhaps I ought to say adieu! This last letter to me makes it terribly plain that what is vomit-making to me is just "rather painful" to you !! (I quote your words!) So if goodbye is just "rather painful," I should say goodbye. It's so *silly* of me to make this fuss, I know, but I'm terribly hurt and somehow *abused* by not knowing that you had become a different person. You are so ABSOLUTE that I imagine you are deeply deeply committed.' There was more. 'PPS: I think too that my "attentions" possibly embarrass you and that you don't like receiving odd parcels at the theatre. This too you'd better answer *truthfully*. Now is the time for it and I won't be any more shattered than I am because I'm prepared to give you up *entirely*, and didn't really expect a letter from you.' The letter ended with an explosion: 'Just the TRUTH Simon – in *simple words!*'

Nor was that all. A second letter, written the following morning ('in my garden'), started: 'Please, please don't remember my birthday. Above all – no gift. Too painful. You don't realise that what I feel is the *deepest humiliation*. Of all your virtues your open frankness was the most unusual and best. Perhaps you took this to excess, as all your friends were privy to everything!!! (Not that I minded who knew what I felt for you and who raised their eyebrows at me.) S, I feel confident in our friendship. But you mentioned nothing about this, and I wonder *how long I've been making an ass of myself*. Do you really think I mind about anything that makes you happy? I don't mind – but I do mind the deception and silence. You allowed one to blunder on and my idea of you inside my head has been false for some time.' Her next paragraph seemed at first to be a non-sequitur, until I realised that it was an example of her extraordinary ability to make the personal epic and the epic personal. 'The worst thing Thatcher has done is to steer a course *humiliating* to the Argentines. She needed to allow them pride, some way they could have accepted, quite early on, which would have kept them their self-respect and honour. An absurd analogy but WISDOM is made up partly of imagination – an understanding of other people's minds, and a realisation that there is a long-changing future ahead for relationships between *people* and *countries*. Without this we destroy all the beauties and the possibilities for a con-tinuous celebration of living one with another.' Scrawled at the bottom of the page was another cry of despair. 'Oh! I'm appalled – I've just squashed an ant on this page – poor little thing. We are all SO ROTTEN.'

'No no no no,' I roared back. 'You have completely misunderstood. Comically so, almost. Rupert is a wayward, slightly jagged young man who has befriended me for whatever – certainly non-carnal – reasons. We play the game of being young West End bloods together (which is far from the case with me, even in jest). We discuss his career, the state of the theatre and sex. It's quite larky and fast. Never, ever, ever, do we touch on any of the areas that you and I do. But then no one does. I said in my last letter, and I meant it absolutely, I had never met anyone like you before, and had never had a friendship – so much more than that, there seems to be no word to describe what I feel about you – a kind of identity, a twinship almost – had never known anything like that before with man woman or child and it was the thing I MOST WANTED – dreamed of all my life. Like you, I always think Oh Peggy would love this; or P would hate it; or I must tell P. The reason I said in the letter that it would be *rather painful* was simply that I didn't want to blackmail you into seeing me, by pitting my pain against yours. To spell it out: I would be utterly bereft if I didn't see you again. Life would lose a great deal of its flavour and not all the Ruperts or Martins or Anguses in the world could make up for it. I love them all, but none of them has that direct line to the very best and deepest part of me that is yours alone. As to the presents: again: nobody has ever been generous in your way. And I have always been embarrassed by gifts, being temperamentally giver rather than taker – like you. But I have never been embarrassed by your gifts. Furious, sometimes, that I can't reciprocate as I'm constantly tempted to. But finding one of your Red

Cross parcels of the soul at the stage door is the most wonderful blessing to the evening. Best of all has been the times we've been to see something together, and then afterwards sat in Redcliffe Square listening to Schubert. Some of those evenings – most of them in fact – have been among the best evenings of my life. I know, Peggy, that for you there's a kind of built-in pain factor, an incompletion. For me it's a very complete experience, one to which I am deeply addicted. As for letters, I have never written a line of a letter to R., nor I imagine shall I. What about, for God's sake? The only people I've ever written to at any length are you and Az, and you can imagine that they're very different kinds of letters. Peggy letters are written only to Peggy, and because of you, they're possibly rather better than they would be; as we saw when I tried to write a piece for the E Standard. When I wrote it for and to you, it was OK. I will get new friends always, for the rest of my life. I'm like that. But how can I persuade you that my feelings for you are based on rock, that I love you very deeply, that the loss of you from my life would be inconsolable; that my feelings for anyone else are nothing to do with my feelings for you. We first met, you and I, just when I was falling in love more deeply than I ever had in my life, and it's extraordinary that there was any emotion left over for another person. The miraculous thing was that my feelings for you were every bit as deep and intense as those for him. The two relationships developed side by side, except that I never wavered with you. I must end this, because I want you to read it tomorrow. But it's only the half of it. Let's talk and meet, P.'

And that finally did it. 'Why did I come to such a different picture via-à-vis Rupert?' she wrote back, immediately '(1) You quoted Du bist die Ruh. (2) You wanted to cancel

America. Perhaps because we haven't been as close in touch recently because of your marathon Faust and your TV and other radio productions and I thought you were getting bored. I'm sending you an envelope so that you can both shop at this man's emporium – they custom-make shirts if that would amuse you, and *get yourself something to wear on your birthday*. I now know what Proust felt when he was writing about "Albertine". He never knew the truth, and it made him *desperate*. So, I love to think of your prancing through the town *à deux* as young bloods: *sweet*. Thank you, dearest Simon. x Peggy x'

Another manifestation of jealousy in rather milder form occurred when, while I was preparing for *On the Spot*, she introduced me over lunch to the aged former secretary of Edgar Wallace, Genia Reissar, with whom she said she had been friends for years, though on meeting they appeared to know nothing whatever about each other. Peggy seemed determined to prevent the other woman from saying anything interesting, or indeed anything at all. She came to the lunch in a hat; no ordinary hat, of course. This was A Hat, a tricorne with a veil in which a number of dead flies appeared to be trapped. From time to time during the course of the conversation, Peggy would flick this veil up with a dramatic action, in an attempt to punctuate, or perhaps to puncture, the stately flow of Genia's reminiscence. On other occasions she would suddenly interrupt her with observations breathtaking in their irrelevance: 'My God!' she would cry, 'there are *carnations* on the table – *carnations*! Can you imagine? Genia: did you know that there were *carnations* on the table?' 'Yes, Peggy,' Genia would calmly reply, and resume the solemn tread of her anecdote. When Genia eventually left to go back to the office, Peggy said 'Ridiculous woman. She had nothing to say.' It has to be observed that women in general did not get a very good press from Peggy. When I spoke to her in glowing terms about Jean Rhys, whom she had represented during that period of late flowering when she wrote *Wide Sargasso Sea*, Peggy dismissed her summarily. 'But,' I said, 'she makes it so clear what women's emotional lives, or some women's emotional lives, are really like.' Peggy said: 'I know what women's emotional lives are like: boring.'

15

Our friendship had by now, after several storm-tossed years, matured into something almost familial. The graph of it evened out. A symptom of this is that in the mid-eighties, after having known Peggy for a full five years, I finally got to know the man with whom she lived. He stayed in the little house she owned in Brighton, so it was essentially a weekends-only affair, though he was sometimes allowed to come up to town to see a show written by one of the clients, and would then stay overnight at Redcliffe Square. His name was Bill Roderick, that much I knew, and he had been an actor, handsome, dashing, a famous ladies' man, but never a star or even a leading player; not in the West End, at any rate. They had had their passionate affair in the forties; Peggy 'stole him,' as she invariably put it, with a look of extreme self-congratulation, from the greatly admired actress, Dorothy Reynolds, and they had lived together thereafter. In 1962 Bill had gone to America with the production of *A Man for All Seasons* (by Peggy's client Robert Bolt). When he returned to England, he had gone back to Peggy and begged her to let him stay with her; he had decided that he no longer wished to act and wanted simply to settle down – though if settling down was your ambition, it is hard to think of a less likely person to do it with than Peggy. 'Out of pity,' she said, she had 'taken him in,' as if he were a stray cat. Once, after I had questioned her about him, she wrote: 'When I got back I asked Bill exactly what had gone wrong with his career. I said we'd been talking about him. He said he knew exactly. He'd had a *wonderful* time in America, not just in New York, but a long long tour, and dreaded coming back. When he did, he was *crushed*. I'd just bought that little house in Brighton and he retired to it, and wouldn't see anyone but me. He found that somehow by going to America for so long – over a year – he'd cut himself off from work, and began to have an inferior complex, that he was *hopeless,* unfit to work and that was that.'

When she spoke of him, which was rarely, it was in terms of exasperation: how she would look up to find him staring at her with adoration, when she felt 'nothing'; how he had no ambitions, no objectives, and wanted only to be with her. This was a claustrophobic horror to her, she said. 'B Rod relies entirely on my visit. You may have trouble with Ziz, but it's NOTHING to what I have. There's no one else in his life but me. He had cut himself off entirely. He has *awful* Meunières disease, an ear infection, which comes suddenly, and flays him to the ground and he's had to lie there for hours till he recovers. He is to have a series of X-rays in the head, blood tests etc. to see exactly what's wrong, and God knows what is. As long as I'm available, he is quite quiescent, but for years now I've had to fit him into my life somehow. I know *you* understand these necessary obligations. It's awful if one thinks that one is *necessary* to someone else's existence – even if they don't ask ANYTHING of one – but just to be there from time to time!' I think she felt guilty about having written this because in a subsequent letter she wrote: 'He has a little money and can manage, and pays his own way. He's really very cheerful and active. I may have given the impression that he wasn't, but I don't talk about my life to anyone, as you know, and it was painful for me to do so with you.'

They always went on holiday together – most often to North Africa, where Peggy would drive, in her notoriously erratic manner, as far into the desert as she dared to go – and the photographs of those trips suggest that they were devoted and cheerful companions. I began to wonder what Bill must feel about me, about my presence in Peggy's life. I hoped that we might meet, as soon as possible, to dissolve any sense of threat he might be experiencing. This was another Obligatory Scene that needed to be played; eventually it was. As when Peggy and Aziz and I had met for the first time, all of us were nervous, but the passions involved were all burning at a much lower temperature, and within minutes it was clear that Bill and I would get on marvellously: we fell into theatrical anecdote, the lingua franca of actors everywhere. What was perhaps more surprising was that Peggy joined in enthusiastically with her own stories of repertory, of Harry Hanson and the fit-up tours. It was clear that those days were the time of Bill's life, but in a curious manner, that they were the time of Peggy's, too. In any other company, even with me when we were on our own, she would dismiss her life as an actress; once, when a friend gave me a photograph of Peggy in a group portrait of a rep production, she said, 'Who is that?' When I told her that it was her – which it unmistakably was, her huge, sexy eyes dominating the whole picture – she flatly refused to believe it, and tried to destroy the photograph. But here, with Bill and me, she happily and unselfconsciously relived those days. He started staying up in town more often – the Meunière's disease made them both feel that it was dangerous for him to be on his own alone in Brighton – and we fairly regularly spent evenings *à trois*; whenever we did, Peggy's basement became a sort of Green Room, awash with theatrical reminiscence. I couldn't have liked it more.

Peggy and I still wrote to each other, but less frequently. We continued sending each other presents, mine now matching and sometimes exceeding hers in splendour. We got interested in paintings, and spent a lot of money in the Francis Kyle Gallery in Maddox Street. We frequently attended his vernissages. Sometimes these could be hair-raising occasions, as Peggy proceeded through the exhibition, gesticulating wildly in response to each painting, quite oblivious of the glass of red wine in her hand. I have a rather subtle water-colour of the Venetian Carnival which I believe has one more red balloon in it than the painter actually painted. We had our favourite artists – at that period Gerald Mynott and Adrian George, unexpectedly soft-focus and pastel, given our taste in other matters – and collected them assiduously and expensively.

We had our outings, too; one of the more memorable the extraordinary occasion on which a cast of French writers (and Snoo Wilson) had been assembled to perform Virginia Woolf's play *Freshwater* in translation, directed by Simone Benmussa. The French writers included Alain Robbe-Grillet, Nathalie Sarraute and, as Alfred, Lord Tennyson, Eugène Ionesco. Peggy was reluctant to attend, but I somewhat disingenuously persuaded her that it would be interesting to find out whether Woolf's play had any value qua play. We went down to the Riverside Studios and found a seat at the top of the bank of seats; Peggy, in her uniquely penetrating tones, offered a running commentary on the 70, 80 and 90-year-old writers, all known to her personally, as each made their appearance. When Ionesco's wife Rosica appeared, Peggy said, in a whisper that could easily have carried across the Thames, 'Ah! La veuve Ionesco!' Ionesco himself had been seated at the side of the stage from the beginning of the evening, wearing a cloak and a large white beard, hooked over his ears. When it came to his turn to speak, he was unable to do so without the aid of the pretty young stage manager who ran her finger along each line as he said it. Despite this help, he was unable to pick up a single cue, and was largely inaudible, to the visible and audible frustration of his fellow-cast members, many of whom were considerably older than him, and most of whom had memorised their parts. Nathalie Sarraute, in particular, eighty-two years old, elegant in her velvet trouser suit and word-perfect, was as impatient as any leading actress with her partner's incompetence. The whole event was enjoyably farcical, enhanced by the occasional appearances of Snoo Wilson's Porpoise, and Peggy's running commentary on the cast: 'Such an interesting writer. *He* loves eleven-year-olds, you know. *She's* written nothing of the slightest merit since 1937. Why does *he* look so old? '

Afterwards, she only wanted to flee, but Ionesco, surrounded by school-children, presumably studying him for O-level, was suddenly full of life and sharp as a button. From amidst the throng of chattering students, he spotted her. 'Peggy!' he cried. 'Peggy! C'est Ionesco! Peggy!' 'Salut, Ionesco,' she said, crossly. 'Téléphonne-moi.' 'Mais à quel numéro?' he cried, to her departing back. In reply, she simply waved gaily at him, without interrupting her hasty retreat. That was the last they ever had to do with each other; he was dead a year later.

On another occasion, she and I went to Luzern together to see the last night of my production of *Così Fan Tutte*. It was a glorious couple of days, the climax of which was our visit to Triebschen, Wagner's summer villa on the Lake, where his wife Cosima was famously serenaded with the *Siegfried Idyll* on her birthday, December 25th, played by a handful of musicians in a boat underneath her window. Peggy was as excited as a child; so was I, but it had a special intensity for her: to a young music lover growing up, as she had, in the early twenties, Wagner's music was modern, just fifty years old, contemporary at only one remove, the giant figure standing directly behind the great composers of her day, Mahler, Richard Strauss, and Schoenberg. We ran round the outside of the villa, peering through the windows – for some reason it was not open to the public that day – and imagined the composer and his family walking in the grounds. 'Triebschen, Triebschen,' she murmured, over and over, 'Triebschen,' as if she were dreaming, and could scarcely believe that she were really here. That night, the night of the performance, she didn't come to supper afterwards with the singers – too painful, she said, though she had loved it – and went straight to bed in the town's main hotel, all carved panels and painted murals.

When we flew back the following day, she was clearly shaken by the whole experience, but as we chatted, in a typical gear-change, she suddenly asked me what the clients thought about Tom Erhardt, her second-in-command. I didn't have much to do with Tom, since his main area of responsibility was the dramatists' foreign rights, but I knew him socially; we got on very well together. 'Do the authors like him?' she asked. I thought they did, and could think of nothing much to say, so, unthinkingly, I said, with early morning doziness, 'Some of them think he might be a little quicker in processing the payments.' This was a stupid and inaccurate extrapolation of a casual remark of Martin Sherman's. 'Who thinks that?' she asked fiercely. I pretended not to remember, but she persisted. 'Who? Who?' Fatally, and with many qualifications, I named Martin. 'How interesting,' she said, and then swiftly changed the subject.

I knew that trouble was brewing. In addition to her formidable constructiveness and generosity, she had a powerfully mischievous impulse, a passion for putting the cat among the pigeons, to which she would give in at the most unexpected moments. Why would she succumb to this impulse today, after what appeared to have been an entirely pleasing, indeed, very moving, little break? I have no idea, even now; but I knew that the moment we got back to London, I must alert everyone involved. I immediately informed Martin, who groaned: Tom at that moment was his greatest champion in the agency, and Martin's foreign earnings were vital to his day-to-day survival. The last thing he needed was to turn Tom against him. I therefore wrote Tom an abject letter which pleaded a complete misunderstanding, apologising to the depths of my being. This manoeuvre just about managed to contain what would otherwise have been an enormous explosion. Peggy had called Tom into her office the moment she arrived there from the airport to tell him that all the clients hated him, none more so than Martin, and that I had given her chapter and verse of his shortcomings. Fortunately, Martin was able to get hold of Tom and disown whatever I was supposed to have said, and my letter backed this up. I lay very low for some weeks; Peggy stalked around in a furious rage for a couple of days; and then it was all over.

On another occasion, I had mentioned to Peggy that Snoo Wilson and I were inspired by the work of a young actress in his play *Loving Reno*, which we were directing together, and that I had thought that she would be brilliant as Wedekind's Lulu. I had a notion that Snoo might make a version of the play, but in a full text, preserving the original two parts, unlike my friend (and her client) Peter Barnes's dazzling condensation of them into the one play that had played in the West End some years before. Peggy seemed to think it a good idea, too; but a couple of days later she called me to say that she'd told Barnes that Snoo and I were planning to steal his play from him. Snoo who didn't know the play at all, had ill-advisedly asked her if he could read a copy of Barnes's version, which was no longer in print. I braced myself for the inevitable kick-back which duly arrived in the form of a letter from Barnes which started 'Dear Simon As you bowl down life's golden pathway . . . ' A letter from me and a lunch were enough to repair that friendship, but the explosion was considerable; anything Peggy touched got bigger, for better or for worse. The single most hurtful thing she ever did to me didn't reach my ears until after her death, when David Hare revealed to me that she had told him that she had more or less put together *Being an Actor* from a shapeless mass of scribbling. I don't know why she felt the need to do that. Denying the possession of any creative gifts herself, she insisted on her powers of insemination: and indeed, she had made many projects happen, and had had any number of good inspirations about subjects, authors, directors and actors (as in the case of *Total Eclipse*). But sometimes other people had good ideas, too, and she was not incapable of claiming them as her own.

The bleak fact was that from the mid-eighties, she was, occasionally at first, and then frequently, prone to confusion and uncharacteristic behaviour, the manifestations of the Alzheimer's disease which gained increasing purchase over her mind. I was only intermittently aware of this, which was, after all, only an amplification of the absent-mindedness which had been such an amusing part of her general manner. I still found it funny when, while I was translating *Jacques and His Master*, she told me about the American production of it by 'that dreadful woman – you know, of course you know – [triumphantly] – Stephen Sondheim.' Somehow I realised that she meant Susan Sontag. 'What did I say?' She couldn't believe it when I told her, and had no recall of it whatever. On another occasion, we went out for lunch, and started talking about Rilke, a great favourite of hers. Suddenly, she wanted to buy me his poems; as it happens, we were eating near Bernard Stone's Poetry Bookshop, then in Floral Street, in Covent Garden. It was an excellent shop, properly eccentric. One of the many jokes which Stone had contrived was to have acquired a wax model, eerily life-like, of Freud, which he had installed behind the counter. Peggy strode straight up to the counter and enquired of the dummy whether he had any of Rilke's poems. There being no reply – though an electrifying silence fell over the shop – she repeated the question more loudly, not without testiness. 'Peggy,' I said, taking her gently by the arm, 'it's a dummy.' 'A dummy?' 'Yes. Of Freud.' 'Well,' she said, after gravely considering this information, 'she's not a very *good-looking* girl, is she?' These eccentric moments came increasingly frequently; but more shocking was her new enthusiasm for being interviewed, a thing she had consistently refused to allow in the past. 'I'm not interesting,' she had always insisted. 'Only the clients are interesting.' Bill's twin brother, along with large numbers of her contemporaries, had died, and perhaps her increasing sense of mortality persuaded her that she should be remembered, although hitherto, she had insisted not only that she wanted no memorial, but that her name should be removed from the firm when she died. The thought never crossed her mind, needless to say, that she might retire and that the firm would carry on without her.

My awareness of these changes in her was only gradual, due to geographical absence. I was spending more and more time out of the country, acting in films and directing. Whenever we met, there was the same warmth, the same tenderness, but our lives no longer coincided; I had moved out of the sphere of her influence, staging plays in Los Angeles and opera in Glasgow. There was nothing she could do to help me, nor did she feel I needed her help any more. She had, she knew, been lucky for me, and she was pleased at my success, but did not feel part of it. Our last great venture together was my biography of Laughton, which she read almost chapter by chapter as I finished it. It united us on many levels – the theatre of her youth; the whole idea of artistic dedication which Laughton embodied for me; Scarborough, where I wrote the book, Laughton's birth-place. She had always loved it, latterly because of the Ayckbourn connection. She loved the book, too, almost without qualification; I think she was surprised that I had managed to do it at all, let alone to do it well. 'The book is quite SPLENDID,' she wrote to me, 'sometimes too rushed, but this gives it the pressure which drives us to read, and not put it down. I am sad I didn't introduce you to Elisabeth Bergner, but I didn't then know you were going to write a book *of this order*.' The book completed another circle. The dedication read: 'This book is for Aziz Yehia (1950-1984).

His love of film, and my love of him, made the book possible,' appending the Emperor Hadrian's address to his soul, in Stephen Oliver's translation: 'Gentle little wandering breath/Of the body the friend and guest/Where now must you look for rest/Pale and naked/Hard as death/Lost without your power to jest?' Peggy wrote to me 'I've managed to snitch an *unfinal* proof of "Chas." I want to say how *really* touched I am that you've dedicated the book to Aziz. I remember all about your friendship, from almost the beginning, and the photo of the two of you is by my bedside. I remember specially the "show" you gave me and the film you both made in Venice (do you have a copy? – if not, ask for it!) Knowing and loving Aziz has made you *what you are* and it's right that the book should be "his" – would this have made him happy?'

It occurs to me that she felt that I had learned my lessons from her, and no longer needed her help. I don't recall that she actually read my next two books; she had died long before the Welles biography appeared. We continued to write to each other but not in quite the same way; and it is remarkable to me that we both stopped keeping the other's letters at the same time, 1986/7.

16

Birthdays were odd events in our lives. The fact that we shared an astrological sign – Gemini – had always pleased both of us, though we were for many years uncertain of the precise day on which the other had been born, and were full of reproaches, some humorous, some more deeply felt, about the omission. In fact, we were so prodigal with gifts all year round that there was not much that we could do to make either birthdays or Christmases different. Certain birthdays, however, have a symbolic power that demand to be distinguished from the usual annual observances. In May 1988 I was sharply aware of the imminence of Peggy's 80th birthday. Her age, give or take a year, was now no longer a secret to the world, though even with me, she was sometimes somewhat wayward about both the year and the day. Once, in the back of a taxi one winter's night as we were on our way to a little exhibition of Diaghilev memorabilia, she had suddenly confided in me that she was born on the same day in the same year as Laurence Olivier, which was simply not the case (he was born on May 22nd 1907, she on May 25th, 1908); it was, however, the first time we had ever talked about her age. 'Are you surprised?' she demanded. 'Are you surprised at how old I am?' I was only surprised at her mentioning it, though of course I said, and truthfully – she was 75 at the time – that she made a mockery of the whole idea of age. She was not consoled by the thought, and that evening, strangely accompanied by wild wind and heavy rain, was a moody, gloomy one. Our visit to the exhibition that night made her even sadder, as if Diaghilev and all he represented belonged to a part of her life that was over. The next time we met, she had cast the mood off, but it was clear that she no longer thought of herself as untouched by age; until very recently she had referred to women much younger than herself as 'that *old* lady'. Not any more. (Once I gave her a jet brooch I had found in a shop in Whitby. She had recoiled from it, saying that black was only suitable for old women: would I not like to give it to my mother – fully fifteen years younger than her.)

So when her eightieth loomed, I was somewhat at a loss to know what to give her for this tremendous anniversary; then it came to me in a flash of inspiration: her hi-fi system, on which we had listened to Schoenberg and Schubert into the small hours of so many mornings, was now hopelessly out of date and unreliable, its automatic action having become eccentric to the point of actually damaging the records, the arm plopping down heavily in the middle of a side. I determined to replace it with a state-of-the-art unit, and to surprise her with it on the birthday itself. She, after all, had given me my first CD player – 'the tin' as she called it – and had marvelled at its, and our, modernity. B. and I duly arrived, triumphant, on her doorstep, with half a dozen cardboard boxes, bent on installing the system ourselves, so that she need not think about it at all, but simply avail herself of all this, to me, self-evidently superior technology. B. and I set about the task of installation, while she and Bill sat and watched, gamely expressing delight and fascination, though evidently bewildered at the strange turn taken by a night they had clearly planned to spend quietly together alone. At some point, in the middle of my frenzy of unpacking and patter and wiring and plugging, I caught sight of them both, and I suddenly knew that it was all a terrible mistake. Peggy didn't want a new hi-fi system; she didn't understand it, and never would. She must, in turn, have caught my look of dismay, because she said, 'It's lovely, dear, such a lovely *surprise*,' which gave me a second wind to finish the job off. Once it was up and working, and I'd put *Rosenkavalier* on the CD player, and we'd all marvelled at it, B. and I made our loving farewells and went, carrying with us the old equipment, which had given Peggy so many years of pleasure, leaving her with the incomprehensible new machine that she would never use. I promised, and gave, tutorials in its use, but we both knew that it was a disaster. I realised how, evermore obsessed with work as I was, running three careers simultaneously, and spending increasing amounts of time abroad, I had lost touch with her; but also how, almost without my noticing it, she had begun to wind down. There was no diminution of love on either side, but passion no longer ruled the roost. The excitement we had felt in each other's company had given way to an immense affection; where we had enthralled each other with our passionate outpourings, we were now often silent; and the electricity that we had generated simply by being in the same room together, making it almost impossible for us to touch each other, had dimmed down to the extent that we would now often sit side by side holding hands like Victorian sweethearts.

I was conscious, too, of a devastating sadness about her, of a fundamental unhappiness, to the extent, I now admit with shame, that when I used to see her making her way down St Martin's Lane, or struggling down the steps at

186

Leicester Square tube station, I would not make myself known to her, fearing both her sadness and her distractedness. Once, just returned from Paris where I had interviewed Peter Brook about Orson Welles, I had come across her sitting alone in the vegetarian restaurant Cranks. When I went up and spoke to her, she recognised me but seemed utterly lost. I told her about my visit. 'You've been to see Orson,' she said dreamily, and couldn't seem to take in my correction, or the purpose of my visit. She kept sighing, and saying how dreadful everything was. Eventually I left her, going away before she had finished her meal; I was so upset that I wept on the way home.

This was only true of chance encounters, however. When we had a formal arrangement to meet, which was still as often as possible, it would be fine; especially if we went to restaurants that we had frequented when we first knew each other. Somehow the familiar circumstances would return her to herself, and she would sparkle and dazzle, as before, though even here there was a noticeable tendency to circularity in her remarks, which would go round and round in a loop – but a wide loop, so this would only happen once or twice during a meal. Once she said to me, 'I keep saying the same things over and over again, don't I?' I said, 'Yes, but it doesn't matter, what you're saying is so interesting, it's well worth repeating.' 'Extraordinary, isn't it? Why do I do that, I wonder?' To this I had no answer, but just held her hand and smiled with tender amusement. She chuckled back. In this later phase of her life, in sharp contrast to her general unhappiness, she laughed a great deal more than she had before, and it was a very different sort of laughter, now girlishly giggly, now deep and rather dirty. She made jokes, which is something that she had never done before, and, even more unprecedented, she would confess herself baffled by things. And she would drink more, not in the way of an alcoholic, but that of a child, guzzling greedily at the wine, as if it were Lucozade or pop.

I had by now broken up with B., and started a relationship with a new partner, M. B. and I had intended to buy a house together, and I had found one almost by accident. Going to interview the late Derek Prouse, a client of Peggy's, as it happens, about Orson Welles, I was astounded to find that he had almost no recollection of the man, though he had translated *Rhinoceros* for him when Welles directed it at the Royal Court with Laurence Olivier. This was – and is – unique in my experience; like Welles or loathe him, nobody came away from him without an anecdote of some sort. 'Large man,' Prouse said, 'smoked cigars. Can't help you much more.' Bereft of further Wellesian openings, I turned the discussion to the house, which I praised. 'Like to buy it?' said Prouse. 'How much?' I said. 'Quarter of a million.' I gulped, but when I consulted my accountant, he thought it was within the bounds of the possible, so I set in motion the process of buying it.

It was at about this time that I broke up with B., and was now stuck with putting up all the money for the mortgage, which I somehow did. I then went to see the place with my new partner, and asked Peggy if she'd like to come along. 'How much is it?' she asked when I went to collect her in the office. 'A quarter of a million.' 'Who's paying for it?' 'I am.' 'Where are you getting the money from?' 'The building society.' 'They're lending you a *quarter of a million?*' 'More or less.' 'Are they MAD?' 'Probably.' She tutted. 'Do you want me to buy it for you?' 'No,' I said, 'no, no, no. I can do this on my own, and I will.' I told her how much I'd earned that year. She seemed appalled. 'They paid you all that money?' 'Yes.' 'What for???' We went off to the Café Pelican in St Martin's Lane, our current restaurant, and there she met M. for the first time. She didn't quite seem to take him in, though she was gracious and funny, if slightly raucous, in her later manner, and we all got tipsy. In the cab to Camden Town, she began to seem a little disorientated, both geographically and historically: she had lived in Belsize Park at her lowest ebb, financially and emotionally, and as we drove further north, some of this seemed to be coming back to her. When we reached the house, we were greeted by Harry Cordwell, Prouse's partner, who had known Peggy well over the years. She was immensely polite, but clearly had no recollection of him whatever. We showed her round the house. She freely scattered comments – 'so dark' – 'what boring wallpaper' – which, given that Harry had decorated the house himself and was in fact an Oscar-winning film set-decorator by profession, were somewhat uncomfortable. At the top of the house she took a tremendous shine to a Japanese print, and became somewhat obsessed by it, till Harry, not without exasperation, gave it to her, which pleased her enormously. She then entered a conversational loop out of which she never emerged until the end of the visit: 'Didn't Sickert live near here?' she asked. 'In Mornington Crescent,' said Harry. 'How extraordinary! To think! Sickert lived here! Where exactly did he live?' 'Mornington Crescent.' 'How extraordinary! Sickert lived here! But where? Where exactly.' 'Mornington Crescent.' 'Mornington Crescent! Who was it who lived there?' 'Sickert.' 'Sickert!!! And where did he live?' etc, etc. Harry, taking this conversational technique for wilful eccentricity, suddenly snapped, 'I've already told you,

189

Peggy: Mornington Crescent.' 'Thank you,' said Peggy, with dignity, 'I simply wanted to know where he lived.' And we went.

17

I left the country for a couple of months; when I got back
I wrote the following letter:

ST PANCRAS WAY LONDON NW1 ORD   28/02/90

Dearest dear P: Staggered back to London at the end of
last week after opening the new play in Los Angeles
then dashing across to Toronto to do a day's filming
with Paul Newman for Jim and Ismail. M. and I were
sitting in the Brompton Brasserie on the Fulham Road,
still gaga with jet lag, when out of the drizzle you and
Bill appeared like a mirage, passing by the window at
which we were sitting, about three inches from our
nose. I gestured feebly to you, but you were gone,
disappeared round the corner. All very dreamlike.

We returned home to the melancholy task of packing. – We decided about six weeks ago that we would
after all move into St Pancras Way and finally leave
Finborough Road. It seemed almost providential – the
Holy Ghost in action, perhaps – that the winds should
sweep the country while we were away and burst the
roof open. The boy who owns the ground floor flat put
in a quick offer for our flat and I quickly accepted it –
£35,000 – only ten more than it cost, but given that it
was on a very short lease which has nearly disappeared

over the eleven years' occupancy, and that the property market is at its least buoyant within living memory, not unreasonable. The offer was conditional on us being out by March 1st, tomorrow, and we will be. Today is our last day here, and very Chekhovian it feels, with walls bare but for the marks of drawing pins and nails, the outline of posters and picture frames spectrally traced in dust and dirt. Packing cases are all around and just the odd big bit of furniture – a desk, or a sofa – stranded in the midst of all the emptiness.

It now begins to look like the shell that we first saw those ten years ago when you and I grabbed a taxi to come and look at it; except that it's now covered in the scars of those ten years. I wear a flat pretty hard, as you can imagine. To be frank, it seems to be coming apart at the seams: cracks everywhere, holes, actual holes, in the ceiling at various points and terrible patches of damp spreading across entire walls, sometimes in the form of suppurating sores bubbling and oozing. No, its day is done, and I don't envy the new chap coming in. But he's an eager young yuppie, and will gaily paper over the cracks and install some upwardly mobile contemporary who will briefly inhabit it on his way to something better, and will hardly notice a thing.

I wonder if the ghosts will make themselves felt? Or am I bringing them with me? They were certainly around in force on Sunday when I started to pack up the photos and the letters. There, really, was my whole life, or at least my love life, and my life in art, and what else is there? Vissi d'arte, vissi d'amore, blah blah blah. Above all in your letters, and Aziz's, but in others, too, that I haven't looked at since I first received them, stretching back to infancy, letters from my grandmother and my mother, even from my father, the whole turbulence swirling around. But the last ten years have been the most intense, the most transforming, the most shattering, the most liberating, and it all happened here, under this roof that you provided for me, Peggy, in the first home I ever had, your gift, and all the people who passed through it with me, Az and J. and B. and now M., and the books that were written here, and the productions planned, and the lines learned and the books read and the pictures contemplated, and the laughs laughed and the tears wept (many, many tears and howls of grief, but many, many laughs and shouts of joy) and the love made, all thanks to you and somehow bound up in you and with you.

I have your letters stored up in box after box and they are the living record of everything we've shared – of what you've taught me – above all the courage to feel – to feel love and to feel art and to give in to it all, and then – your words engraved on my heart – then to pick up the bill. Well, I have learned that, but before I did it was you who picked up the bill for me on so many occasions, and I don't mean money, though god knows, you've poured that out in lavish quantity. No, you have made me reckless of cost in the emotional sense, because your feelings seemed to be an account that could never be overdrawn.

People keep asking me to talk to them about you – journalists, television people. John Lahr was the latest. I keep saying no. They can make of you whatever version they choose, but I refuse to reduce the you I love to their scale. Let them talk about your position in the literary history of our times; they always miss the point of who you are. I won't collaborate with them in making you a media icon.

I hope you'll come to see us in St Pancras Way. The dark Victorian place that you saw that day we went together to look at it is already different, now that the heavy furniture is gone and some of the wallpaper painted over. M. has wonderful instincts for the placing of furniture etc., but the crucial thing for both of us is that we should choose everything together and – your advice to me on moving into Finborough Road, largely unheeded, of course – there'll be nothing in it that we don't want, really want. I found a book in California, where else?, called *Feng Shui, the Japanese Art of Placement*, which reveals the laws, no less, of arranging rooms, and we shall abide by them. It's a new life, in every way. The last six months with M. have been wonderful, a revelation in some ways, but not without difficulties, the difficulties that anyone who has the madness to embark on a relationship with me has to endure, and some that come from his own passionate, dramatic temperament. But it's the first time that I've really truly tried to live a life *à deux* and it seems to me it's as heroic an undertaking as anything I've ever done. Darling, can we meet over lunch or something? Best would be if you'd come to the house, perhaps for early supper. Whatever's easiest. I'll phone.

Much much love

Then I was off again, to set up *The Ballad of the Sad Café*, which I was to direct for Merchant Ivory; I returned very briefly to meet a potential director of cinematography for the film. Peggy meanwhile, had become known to a far wider public in a BBC2 documentary, *Peggy and Her Writers*, made, against my advice (for obvious reasons) by Rosemary Wilton. The end result was extremely tactful and constitutes the only extended filmed record of Peggy in existence, so I was grateful to have seen it; but it is in no way representative of her at her prime, which lasted until only a couple of years before television got round to her. The implied criticism in that last phrase is unjust; at her prime she would never have dreamed of going on television, except to talk about one of her writers; certainly she would never ever have consented to the making of a programme about herself. 'I'm not interesting,' she said over and over. 'Only the writers are interesting.' But now, in her old age, surrounded by and filled with intimations of mortality, she wanted, I believe, to feel that she had done something; she began to dwell more in the past than the present; the future – always an inspiration to her – had become opaque, or dense with the unthinkable. She started to keep her own clippings, all of the (very favourable) reviews of *Peggy and Her Writers* lovingly gathered together and dated.

ST PANCRAS WAY LONDON NW1   11.IV.90

Dearest P: Nick Hern tells me they've sent you *Shooting the Actor*, as requested. The Introduction introduces it – no need for me to say any more, except that for some reason it was the hardest thing I've ever written. I think it had something to do with the tricky business of transcribing dictated thoughts; more importantly because I had to try to bring out what was really happening, rather than merely recording the ten million tiny details which make day-to-day work on a film such a night-

195

mare. – When you read the first draft of *Being an Actor*, you said it made you fall in love with the theatre all over again. I don't think there's any chance of your saying that about this. Perhaps I'm just older; or perhaps film-making can't have any romance for an actor. Perhaps, too, I'll take it all back when I direct my own first, any moment now. Pre-production starts next Wednesday. We have no leading man (the one we cast is trying to do two jobs at once) and the financial arrangements are vague to the point of obfuscation, but Ismail is producing, and somehow I have faith that things will fall into place. He seems to make films the way he makes his famous curries – on an impulse, with a minimum of preparation and to no known recipe. I think the only thing for me to do is to relax and enjoy it, and just hope that everyone else can . . .

The Documentary: you looked ravishing and talked horse sense. Typical. Wonderful to have it.

Much love S

I was back in England in the New Year, 1991, in January, editing *The Ballad of the Sad Café* and preparing *Carmen Jones*. I made an entry in my diary on 22 January.

Lunch with Peggy. First time I've seen her in over a year. Great anxiety, not knowing what to expect. I've had personal experience of the circular conversations, which are maddening but not actual proof of Alzheimer's, the word which is darkly muttered by many. Will she even remember who I am? Is she completely gaga? – Not a bit of it. Delightful lunch at Sheekey's as she remembers all kinds of tiny details – the first time we ate at Sheekey's and the unfortunate incident with the emetic oysters;

the conservatory in my house, and what am I going to do with it. – We talk about Thomas Mann, Aleister Crowley (PR: 'Was he a fake?' SC: 'I don't know: a charlatan who sometimes hit on the truth, I should say. Like all the rest of us.' 'Well THANK YOU!') – I mention *Ballad*. She's terribly keen to see it, asks about Vanessa. Touches the top of her brow with a questioning expression, as if to say: 'Is she mad?' 'Oh completely,' I say. 'Stupid?' 'No, not at all!' 'Intelligent, then?' 'Intelligent with a poet's intelligence, not that of a scientist.' A pause, then: 'Didn't I play her once?' 'She played you.' 'Oh yes, that was it. Was she any good as me?' 'She missed you by a mile.' 'What do you *mean*?' 'She played you as all benevolence, radiating kindness and sweetness and light.' 'God *God*. Has she ever MET me?' The usual put-down of Ayckbourn – 'They only get worse, don't they, dear?' – of Hampton and of Hare. 'Have you seen Hare recently?' I asked. 'I probably have – obviously not a very memorable encounter.' Allusions to LORD McKellen. She's completely on the ball, but in her own world. She's lost touch completely with the theatre and with new writing; speaks only of the past – hers and literature's. There was always a touch of this, and it was one of the things that made her so extraordinary as an agent for new writing – everything was judged against the masters. Now though she seems to have a gentle contempt for anything that's going on. Partly, of course, she can't focus on it or remember it if she did manage to focus. But she's the same Peggy, with a skittishness which is new. Deep sadness about Jill Bennett – 'I went to her funeral – or do I just think I did? I have a strong impression of it; but I'm not at all sure I was there.' Tom says Peggy keeps forgetting who Colin Chambers is. He's writing a book about her and is therefore around the office rather a lot. 'Who is he, dear? Is he an accountant?' 'He's writing a book about you.' 'Is that a good idea?' 'Yes, wonderful.' 'He's writing a book about me. How TOUCHING. But who is he? Is he an accountant?' And they're off again.

In March 1991, Bill Roderick's health was declining further, despite two operations. Our doctor, Marisa Viegas, visited Bill at the flat in Redcliffe Square, and found him to be desperately ill. She also thought that Peggy was unwell, and certainly in the throes of senile dementia. I protested at the brutality of the diagnosis: she was far more often lucid than otherwise, I insisted, and still did a full working day at the office, which was technically true, though she was inclined to sleep for quite a large proportion of the time. Marisa countered that whatever the truth of that, she was not capable of nursing a dying man. She immediately arranged for a live-in nurse, who lasted exactly twenty-four hours before Peggy drove her out of the house. She had never shared her domestic responsibilities with anyone else, and didn't mean to start now.

Just as all this was brewing, fate casually dealt another blow: the office at Goodwin's Court went up in flames. Peggy took this strangely symbolic act with surprising calm. My diary entry for March 10 reads:

Bill is dying – a matter of days only, says Marisa. Peggy tells me the same thing, completely matter of fact, then wonders if he might recover. But she doesn't seem at all deluded. 'Marisa's good', I say. 'I'm not so sure,' she replies, 'she's got him in that nursing home and she owns it – making a fortune.' (This is absolutely not true). I meet her in the charred remains of the office. It looks like Hitler's bunker. The walls are scabby and blistered, the stench of smoke is everywhere. She's rather pleased when I tell her that I read about it in *The Times*; even more pleased when I tell her the headline: LITERARY BLAZE IN ONE OF BRITAIN'S LEADING AGENTS' OFFICE. 'I'm not so sure I like "one of",' I said. "Exactly", she replied, and really laughed. We went off to eat. She wolfed her haddock and poached egg as she rarely wolfs anything, preferring normally to pick. 'Convalescent food,' I said. 'Why not?' she cried, forking it down in record speed. Then she paused. 'Who do you think did it? The fire, I mean?' 'I can't imagine,' I said, truthfully. 'I have a good idea,' she said, 'but I'm not telling anyone.' 'Who?' I said, conspiratorially. 'I think it was Kureishi,' she replied. 'Hanif?' I said. 'But why? Did you ever turn him down?' 'No, never, I've never read anything he's written, but one day at Hampstead we passed each other in a corridor and he looked at me with such hatred! It was terrible – a terrible look. Do you think it might have been him?' 'I shouldn't think so,' I said, and she seemed to believe me for a moment, but she kept coming back to it: 'Do you think it WAS Kureishi?' – I mentioned the possibility of making a film of Mann's first story *Little Herr Friedemann*, about the hopeless love of a man of restricted growth for a beautiful woman, and she was transported with delight and practical plans – who could play it? I told her about Cork, the dwarf I had just directed in *The Ballad*, and said he'd be perfect, and she was pleased at the thought, but then said: 'I think YOU should play it. Of course, you'd have to have very tall actors – very very tall actors. Is that a good idea?' We parted most happily.

Bill Roderick finally died. I escorted her, with everyone from the office, to the Crematorium at Golder's Green.

Diary: 24.IV.91: Bill's cremation: 'Where are we going? Oh my god. How are we getting there? Who has reserved the car? Will it be on time?' Constantly checking her keys. But the drive there was all right – quite jolly. Bill's last words, she tells me, were: be nice to my family. 'Well, I'M DOING MY BEST.' Then as we approached the crematorium, waves of horror. 'Oh my god, how dreadful, how dreadful.' She pulls herself together, though, and is very gracious to everyone, asking me quite audibly of the fellow mourner to whom she is speaking: 'who is this?' They're all very nice to her. Ridiculous sermon by Bill's brother-in-law ('relationship is what is at the centre of our life – relationship between man and man, man and god, and Bill was always involved in this relationship.' WHAT?) – and the absurd Ortonian spectacle of the coffin trundling into the flames. P. grasped the pew, and my hand, but seemed not excessively moved. Oscar Lewenstein, now a tiny white-haired gnome, has showed up; we all travel back in the same car. Within minutes we're roaring with laughter. She seems perfectly OK, though worried about everybody finding the Pelican, where she's decided to have the wake. She's also convinced that Bill's sister Hope – about whose name much laughter – is furious that Bill's left everything to Peggy.

We arrive at the Pelican; she and I go to our respective lavatories. She emerges with full-face make-up, the first time I've seen her like this for months. It was one of the first things to go. People start arriving, she presses food and champagne and some mad cocktail that she and I have discovered onto everyone: they loathe the cocktail (Pelican Fizz: Pernod and champagne – tastes as if someone has dropped a gob-stopper into a glass of bubbly) but make merry conversation. Bill's other sister – the Rev. Basil's wife – asks me 'Did you really like Bill?' and seems satisfied by my reply that I did: he was like someone from a vanished era, and talking to him made the theatre of the past come alive. Peggy nods nostalgically (though this is the side of him that maddened her most of all). D. Hare arrives, tense and sombre, quickly realising that it's not that kind of a do, and starts to join in the general merriment. Peggy tries to explain who he is, demands of me – quite openly, in front of Hare himself – what he's written, which are his FAMOUS plays. I reel a few off, then – since it's the Rev. Basil to whom we're talking – happily hit on *Racing Demon*. His face lights up. Is that, he asks, the same play as *See How They Run*, Bunny Hare? 'Different Hare,' says David, through tight but amused lips. People go. Peggy looks a little sad and slightly bewildered, then panics over paying, though all that has obviously been sorted out by Tom & the girls from the office, who can barely conceal their impatience with her. But, at the end, she says: 'Bill would have loved this.' And he would have done. On the way out, Hare and I walk up the road together. He tells me that she phoned him at the weekend and actually wept – the first time she's ever done that in his presence. She was, he says, just like a human being, saying she'd just have to somehow live through it. She tells him that Bill was very calm at the end. She asked him whether he was frightened. No, he'd said, he was all right. 'I suppose,' Peggy said to David, 'death prepares you for death.' David said to me: 'And then one remembered why she was so extraordinary.'

I took her to *The Ballad of the Sad Café* and she was fascinated by it, alert and full of opinions about everything. 'Thank god,' she said, 'to get out of the office and all this DEATH.' 'It's the antidote,' I said, 'art.' 'Yes,' she said, profoundly agreeing. She made M. and me eat with her, and had a lager, which she knocked back with relish, as she gobbled up her tarte tatin. She now favoured sweet things, children's food. The next day I took her to *Carmen Jones* (we had a cake before) and her panic and agitation in the office when I picked her up subsided. Martin Sherman had arrived shortly after me. She'd been so distracted that when I said, 'Here's Martin, Peggy,' she refused even to look at him: 'I'm too upset to talk to anyone. I don't want to speak to him' (this right in front of him). He beat a baffled but immediate retreat. She loved *Carmen Jones*, though between the first two acts she said to me that she thought the approach somewhat trivialised *Carmen*. But she warmed to it, and by the end was really full of admiration for it and all the cast. At the interval we had an ice-cream; apple charlotte flavour. She gobbled it up, once it had thawed, and after I'd churned it up a bit for her. Then she went off into the evening, insisting that I had work to do, and she'd find her own cab.

'She feels very cold all the time,' I told my diary.

18

In August, I went away to Greece for three weeks. When I returned, there was a message from David Hare telling me that Peggy was in the London Clinic; he had been looking after her, since it was evident that she was too ill to look after herself. From now on we shared the burden. We became very close in an almost fraternal way as we watched the final decline of the woman we had both loved so deeply, and who had loved us so unstintingly – this woman who had chosen us. The moment I got the message I called her, and then went to see her.

7.IX.91: Telephone conversation: who is this? Simon. Oh. How are you? Well, it's very early in the morning. Where are you? Kentish Town. Why? I live there. Where is it? North of London. Why are you there? And so on. Can I go home? Not for a while. Why not? You're ill. What's the matter with me? It's your legs. But I want to pee. I want to pee badly. Call the nurse. NURSE! NURSE! She doesn't hear me. – I ring off, ring back, tell the nurse she wants to pee. It's a catheter, apparently, makes her feel she wants to pee. I go in. Peggy in hospital: little lost struggling figure. Pain in legs: sheets lifted up. She tries to draw up her night-gown. My first glimpse of her: absolutely naked ancient person. Call nurse in to dress her: she wouldn't like it, waking up and finding me staring at her naked body. Face bruised. Hands swollen. Clawing the air. Our conversation: why am I here? Why am I here? You're ill. How? It's your legs. Do they hurt? No. Why am I here? Can I go home? No, not for a little while. Then numbers: 8431, 8431. Key in hand. She can read the label: it says CONCORDE. Breathing laboured. She falls asleep however. I go. Next time with David. She doesn't speak; strange movements with hand. What's she trying to do, he asks. I realise. Wants to brush her hair back. A good sign, I say. Another time with Willy Russell. She talks about South Africa. I like South Africa. Where are we? Are we in South Africa? I want to go home, etc. Then: I want to pee. Go ahead, I say. Where? Where you are. I don't have to pee in the corner? No. Where then? Just where you are. That's rather *unusual* isn't it? Peggy herself again, for the first time. More imperious. Asks something about the end. Repeats it. What does it mean? Next time more together again. – Drank some orange juice that morning. After a while says to nurse: enough of the orange juice: what about breakfast? Last visit: asleep, with oxygen mask. I go up corridor to speak to nurse. Willy rushes back: she's calling for you. Hello darling it's Simon. Hello darling. How are you? I'm fine. How are you? I'm so feeble. Weak. Of course. No pain? No. Are you busy? Yes, yes, very busy. That's all right then. Bye bye then darling. Bye bye, I say, laughing at the sweetness of it. I go. Later message from Hare: it's looking black. We speak: she's rallied before, I say. Exactly, he says. I go to supper, he goes to bed. Coming home, message on machine from hospital; she's gone. I call David. We're there, with M., in minutes. She's perfectly still. The first time I've seen her still, ever, even in sleep.

David and M. and I sat in the adjacent room for a little while, and then I went back home with M. and played the music Peggy and I played so often. At the first note of the Presentation of the Silver Rose from *Rosenkavalier*, I wept uncontrollably, of course, but they were tears of gratitude as well as grief, of relief as well as mourning. The humiliation was over for her; for me, the memory was bright and burnished.

She had died on September 4th. The next day, and the days after that, were not good. On the 8th, Hugh Whitemore, one of the many clients with whom Peggy had fallen out, called me and left an extraordinary message. 'I just wanted to say how devastated one was by Peggy's death. One had no idea – and of course one should have realised – how much she meant to one. I know how much you meant to her – and I just wanted to say how grateful I am for that. Also to express a degree of envy that you knew her so well, and I never did.' His message made me think all over again – a quick glimpse of the letters two days before had suddenly brought it all back to me, the scorching intensity of feeling – how much I DID mean to her. I wept, and wondered what was it in me that evoked such passion, and how could I live up to whatever it was.

The days got heavier. Both David and I felt kicked in the stomach; the antidote was to plan the service at the crematorium, an easy enough task, after all, the only difficulty knowing what to leave out. One thing was for sure: there would be no God in it. I never heard Peggy speak of God or invoke him or refer to him in any way. Art and Feeling were, quite literally, her gods. David and Christopher Hampton and I devised a programme of music and words that broadly covered her passions: the Schubert String Quintet, the Presentation of the Rose, Schnozzola Durante singing 'Start Off Each Day With A Song' (she went to every performance he gave at the London Palladium in the 50's, and loved his feet: 'Those little paws!'); Japanese music – 'The Tenderness of Cranes' – for the coffin's journey into the incinerator; and Jessye Norman singing the final of Strauss's Four Last Songs as we left the chapel. These were to be interspersed with writing: by Maupassant, Proust, Tom Hopkinson, Cocteau, Rimbaud, Shakespeare. Curiously there was nothing from a play; Shakespeare was represented by a Sonnet: no. LXXI: When I am dead, no longer mourn for me/Than you shall hear the surly sullen bell.

The chapel overflowed with the many people to whom Peggy mattered, producers, managers, directors, writers, publishers, actors, the aristocracy of the profession. She had warred with many of them, fallen out definitively with not a few, provoked them all. Now here they were, at her funeral. They all seemed properly awed at the stilling of her voice, at the quenching of her fire. David and I were, I suppose, the mourners-in-chief. I was barely coherent, shaking violently through the music, trembling, wobbly-voiced, as I read the Maupassant, taking deep breaths to fight off tears: 'We must feel. That is everything. We must feel as a brute beast filled with nerves feels, and knows that it has felt and knows that each feeling shakes it like an earthquake. But we must not say that we have been so shaken. At the most we can let it be known to few people who will respect the confidence.' Willy Russell and Vanessa Redgrave read Cocteau and Gorki and Virginia Woolf; David read from the end of Tom Hopkinson's *The Third Secretary's Story*, the companion story to *Over the Bridge*, the one I had read on radio, thanks to her, eleven years earlier, at the very start of our friendship. Its last words had a special resonance for her, and for David, and for me: 'The shape of the world changes and the organisation of its surface changes, the people who inhabit the surface disappear. With them, their memories vanish too. A single generation is enough to obliterate all record. Two generations – and even remembrance may be gone. The memories of those who wish to recall, betray them. Already perhaps there is no one in the world who remembers the wife of an English doctor, except me; and I remember her only dimly; and I shall not remember her for long.' The last piece of text, which I read, was Christopher Hampton's translation of Rimbaud's great poem in which he imagines Verlaine speaking of him: 'He lifted up drunks in the black streets. He had the pity a bad mother has for small children. He moved with the grace of a little girl at catechism. He pretended to know about everything, business, art, medicine. I followed him, I had to!'

Then the last of the Last Songs – the Eichendorff setting, *Im Abendrot*, In the Sunset Glow – in all its sumptuous harmony, valleys descending about us, larks rising hazily up-wards, the solo violin introducing death's serene invitation. 'Wie sind wir wandermüde. Ist dies etwa der Tod?' – 'We are weary with wandering. Can this be death?' As Jessye Norman's huge voice, which Peggy and I had heard so often together in the flesh, tapered slowly toward the final lines, and the flutes took the poem's two larks higher and higher up into the Empyrean, an unplanned moment of theatre occurred: the back door of the chapel swung open to reveal a sun-drenched garden and lawn. Perhaps this vision of nature and life after the sombre ceremony of death is standard, a normal part of the service (though certainly nothing like it had happened at Bill's cremation); in conjunction with the Strauss it proved overwhelming.

It was, as so often, the necessary relief, the first full giving-in. Within minutes we were gathering in groups to talk about Peggy; and inevitably that led to laughter. We repaired to a room at the Café Royal, and drank champagne and ate canapés and talked and laughed ourselves out. And that was it. I still had something to do. Along with our solicitor, Laurence Harbottle, I was Peggy's executor. I had the keys to the flat in Redcliffe Square, which I had not seen for over a year; whenever Peggy and I had met lately, it had been in a restaurant or at the office. I went, one wet September evening, and let myself in. Everything was exactly as it had always been, even down to the odd discarded stocking. Impossible to believe that Peggy would not emerge with a bottle and some pâté from Hobbs, that the air would not soon be filled with Schumann or Schoenberg, that the cat would not make its secretive way across the floor in search of food. The air was still fragrant with Mitsouko. I walked shakily through the flat. By the bedside were the books she was reading when she went to hospital – Claire Tomalin's *The Invisible Woman*, John Cheever short stories. On the bedside table was a small framed photograph of Aziz and me. I knew it was there; I had seen it a hundred times, but it was suddenly unbearable. I picked it up and took it away.

The official reason for my visit was to make my choice of her books. This was stipulated in her will; she also left me £1,000. There were a couple of other individual bequests, to David, to Tom and the girls, but the bulk of her fortune (and that was what it proved to be; over three million pounds) was left 'to benefit writers'. In the next few weeks, Laurence Harbottle and I decided how to interpret that phrase; meanwhile, I had to choose from the thousands of books around me. Many of the ones I took I had given her: a complete revised Proust; various books on art; biographies. I took some of the novels that she loved but which I had never read: by Montherlant, for example, or Feuchtwänger, her great moderns. I took a few plays signed by the authors, including some of Edward Bond's inscribed with poems, her copy of John Osborne's *A Better Class of Person* – inscribed 'to Peggy, a better class of agent' – and the books from the bedside. Only about twenty books, in all. I also took a couple of bibelots which I had given her – a fierce Chinese dog, an American Indian rainmaker – and a couple of bottles of wine, to toast her with, one of which I opened there and then.

As I rummaged slowly among the books, I found, hidden, or merely forgotten, behind one of the shelves, Joe Orton's hand-written Morocco diary (which Peggy had lent me to read at the beginning of our friendship). Digging further, I discovered something infinitely more exciting and revealing: two exercise books bound in wallpaper filled with writing in Peggy's frisky, imperious hand. At first they seemed to be a diaries; but on examination proved to be commonplace books, in which she had written down passages from books which had struck her as relevant either to life or to playwriting – or indeed to both, since she always insisted on their interdependence. There were poems by Verlaine and Baudelaire, pages from Saint-Exupéry, Péguy and St Isaak of Syria, notes on Freud and Jung, Sartre and Bion. There were summaries of Aristotle's *Poetics* and notes on dramatic construction from Howard Lindsay ('1.

Organisation of the emotions. Engage the emotions of the audience towards one or more characters. 2. Story progress. The speed of the story must have direct relationship to the depth of the emotional response 3. Dramatisation. Don't tell us, show us. Have it happen on stage.')

Anyone who knew Peggy or had worked with her would recognise these quotations; they filled her letters and her conversation. But they were not reach-me-down; she had inscribed them not just on the page but in her heart; they had become part of her. The date of the first book is July 1952 – the time when she had started to become involved in management, and was edging towards becoming an agent. She had obviously trained herself, both in dramaturgy and in the crystallisation of her own emotional philosophy; she had consciously educated her sensibilities. The discovery of these books only made Peggy seem more remarkable even than I had thought her to be. Her extraordinary gifts and her inimitable spirit had not sprung from nowhere, was not a mere gift of nature; she had taken stock of herself and the craft to which she devoted her life in the most rigorous fashion, taming a temperament which was in many ways opposed to the discipline she sought to impose on it. Small wonder that sometimes the wild creature that she was au fond would assert herself from time to time, lashing out, or racing headlong after the object of her desires.

One of the most extraordinary of the quotations in her commonplace books is from Saroyan – I have not been able to determine from which book – and it is a remarkable summary of her strange non-canonical form of existentialism:

Everyman is a good man in a bad world. Everyman himself changes from good to bad, back and forth all his

210

life and then dies. But no matter how or why or when a man changes, he remains a good man in a bad world, as he himself knows. All his life a man fights death and then at last loses the fight always having known he would. Loneliness is Everyman's portion, and failure. The man who seeks to escape from loneliness is a lunatic. The man who does not know that all is failure is a fool. The man who does not laugh at these things is a bore. But there is a meaning to a man. There is a meaning to the life Everyman lives. It is a secret meaning, and pathetic were it not for the lies of art, for which Everyman must be grateful, as he himself knows. For the lies tell him to wait. They tell him to hang on. No man's life means more than another's, as each man himself knows. The luckiest man is the one who enjoys his portion, but no man is very lucky, for every man's portion is equally poor, and putting up with it is painful. Most of his experience cannot be enjoyed. Most of it hurts and some of it kills and inflicts the wounds that stop him in his tracks. No man cares about anyone but himself. No man loves anyone but himself. A woman is grateful to a man who plunges her into a passion for herself, and so it is with a man. Together they come to a fine and ferocious feeling about themselves, and call it love. But is only another way for them to forget for a moment the nagging truth that it is meaningless to live.

A man's needs are few, his desires many, but the need and the desire are the same, love. But love like money is a dangerous thing and the possession of it does peculiar things to a man, and the want of it does terrible things to a man.

To be loved is to be accepted. To love is to accept. It is probably good but probably impossible to accept. To reject is probably bad but probably natural. Man is not beautiful, but the yearning for beauty is beautiful, and man's true beauty, which is unrejectable, is failure, extreme and absolute. His effort to love is a comic thing. Everything a man does is for love, and therefore hopeless and futile, and therefore beautiful and comic.

All his life everything a man does he seems to have done before. He is forever kissing the same mouth, embracing the same woman, looking into the same eyes which will not yield their secret. A man wears the same face all his life, but sees a stranger every time he shaves. He inhabits the same body all his life but himself is never the same in it. Everywhere he goes is a place he knows and does not know, home and nowhere, his own place and nobody's at all.

He comes to birth and goes to death. He comes to desire and goes to pain. For Everyman is too much for himself. Everyman is too many men to contain and control, as he himself knows.

A man simply doesn't know. He doesn't know anything. A man simply does not live, he is lived, and not simply. He is lived foolishly and in everlasting indefiniteness and confusion. But he is always a man, a thing in shoes, a better worshipper of shoes than of god, a pale, hairless thing of anxious ill-health, made of poison and dreams, quivering fears and roistering delusions.

Ho for tomorrow! Is the cry of his heart. Or Ah for yesterday! Now is always his time of pain, torment and torture. Today is the terrible time. This moment is hell.

A man's coming and going is lonely and secret, and yet all his coming and going seems to be with companion strangers who fell in beside him because they were coming and going too. A man has no fears. He is instantly and continuously himself for he cannot cease to be who he is until he is dead.

There was some of all this going on in Peggy, a sense of the paradoxical, an almost mystical awareness of the delusory nature of love and of life. Her one encounter with what might be called the religious dimension was with Jiddu Krishnamurti, the reformed Theosophist who preached against organised religion, and in favour of inner experience. His injunction to 'silence the ceaseless chattering of the mind' impressed her deeply, as had – typically – his sudden statement to his disciples at Brockwood Park, many of whom had returned year after year, that 'You haven't understood a word that I've said to you; not a word.' Peggy believed that life must be embraced in all its tragic harshness; that was the source of her capacity for joy. I recall her turning to me after we had just seen *Jean de Florette* and saying, with deep approval: 'The French are so pitiless.' When we were preparing her funeral, a famous couple of lines from Pater's *Studies in the Renaissance* kept coming to me: 'A counted number of pulses is given to us only of a variegated dramatic life. How may we see in them all that is to be seen in them by the finest dramatic pulses? How can we pass most swiftly from point to point, and be present always at the focus where the greatest number of vital forces unite in their purest energy? To burn always with that hard, gem-like flame, to maintain this ecstasy, is success in life.' By those lights, her success in life was as great as that of any human being I have met or hope to.

Once, when we were talking about Venice, I happened to remark how wonderful it would be to have one's ashes sprinkled there, in the great cemetery of San Michele. 'Yes,' Peggy murmured with great intensity, 'wonderful.' For reasons that I am unable to fathom, I have not yet performed that simple ceremony. Perhaps I feel that it would be a final farewell. If so, I cannot bring myself to perform it. I don't know that I ever shall.